The Sociology Game

THE SOCIOLOGY GAME

An Introduction to Sociological Reasoning

R J Anderson
J A Hughes
W W Sharrock

LONGMAN
London and New York

Longman Group Limited
Longman House, Burnt Mill, Harlow
Essex CM20 2JE, England
Associated companies throughout the world

Published in the United States of America
by Longman Inc., New York

First published 1985

BRITISH LIBRARY CATALOGUING IN PUBLICATION DATA

Anderson, R.J.
   The sociology game: an introduction to
   sociological reasoning.
   1. Sociology
   I. Title   II. Hughes, J.A.   III. Sharrock, W.W.
   301′.01   HM24
   ISBN 0-582-29641-2

LIBRARY OF CONGRESS CATALOGING IN PUBLICATION DATA

Anderson, R.J.
   The sociology game.

   Bibliography: p.
   Includes index.
   1. Sociology.   I. Hughes, J.A., 1941–
II. Sharrock, W.W. (Wes W.)   III. Title.
HM51.A535   1985   301   84-19442
ISBN 0-582-29641-2

Produced by Longman Group (FE) Ltd
Printed in Hong Kong

CONTENTS

ACKNOWLEDGEMENTS

As always there are numerous people to whom we owe debts of various kinds, and in this case the unsung heroes of introductory sociology courses we have taught over the years must rank high on our priorities. Also, thanks to our colleagues whether they agree with what we have tried to say or not. In particular we would like to extend thanks to Dave Francis, Joke Esseveld, and Ron Eyerman who all read various drafts and offered perceptive comments. Thanks, too, to Maeve Conolly and Heather Salt who rendered valuable secretarial assistance. And, finally, thanks to our families who have had to bear, not always with fortitude, the vagaries of mood that writing seems to generate.

INTRODUCTION

Most introductory texts aim at distinctiveness, and this is no different. For us its distinctiveness lies in its attempt to emphasise sociology's problems and arguments, a conception which is often at odds with more traditional portrayals of the discipline. In these sociology is presented as a body of knowledge, theories, and findings, about society or social life. Although not necessarily subscribing to the view that sociology can be like the natural sciences in all respects, nevertheless, the traditional conception normally urges that it should aspire to meet the standards of knowledge set by the natural sciences by producing descriptions of and theories about society and social life which are rigorous, empirical grounded, and true. By these kind of standards sociology falls far short. Its theories are, by comparison, vague, loosely formulated, imprecise, its methods crude, and its findings non-cumulative. Though many, and plausible, reasons are offered for this state of affairs, the fact of the matter is that sociology falls far short of its advertising, and opens itself to mockery from the more well-established disciplines, dissatisfaction among its students, and a more or less constant need for self-apology.

However, in emphasising sociology's problems and arguments we do not intend to denigrate it: on the contrary. What we want to show is that the difficulties it faces are real and important ones. We want to claim that more can be said for sociology than its detractors allow, but less than its overenthusiastic advocates urge. For those who are interested in sociology there is much to do and many challenges to meet. In our view there is no need constantly to justify the discipline and no reason at all why it should be made endlessly accountable. Good sociological work has as much academic and intellectual worth as good work in any discipline. If there is a lot of bad and inconsequential work in sociology, so there is much to be found in other disciplines. To adapt a remark Theodore Sturgeon made about science fiction: 75 per cent of sociology is rubbish, but then 75 per cent of everything is rubbish. For us the failure of sociology to meet the aspiration alluded to earlier is more a testament to the difficulty of the subject than it is to the poor quality of its practitioners, its undeserved intellectual status, its immaturity, or whatever.

To put the matter bluntly, sociology is a mess: a fact which does not deter us one jot. Its arguments fail to come to firm conclusions, its inquiries do not close off avenues of dispute, its studies do not fit together in neatly cumulative ways, and it has no fundamentals to speak of: features which, we hasten to add, typify more disciplines, including scientific ones, than one might imagine. There is, we suggest, more to learn from sociology's mistakes and its problems, especially that they are difficult problems, than its few successes. Our account, then, will emphasise the extent of the disagreements in the discipline and the shortcomings of many of its ideas. In doing so we shall treat sociology not as a set of perspectives, the currently popular way of presenting the discipline, nor as a corpus of knowledge, nor as a set of findings about society and social life, but as a set of arguments to be reviewed and thought about.

One immediate consequence of this emphasis is that it draws attention to the hesitant quality of its ideas and to the fact that there is still much to do before we can feel confident that what the discipline has to say meets the highest possible standards of intellectual rigour. Another, and equally important, consequence of stressing the argument character of the discipline is that it points to the choices available in sociology. In our view, students are too often given the impression that one perspective, one paradigm, one approach is the way to the truth about society: that one of the tasks is to find the one approach, the one theory which will tell the whole story, so to speak. The past twenty or so years have seen a number of perspectives come and go as occupants of this position. Some years ago it was Functionalism, followed by Conflict Theory and, more contemporaneously, Marxism. During the hegemony of a perspective, other approaches are generally treated as but poor and deficient attempts to formulate a proper strategy for the discipline, which too often means that students fail to examine them properly as serious alternatives. Not only does this run the risk of producing an impoverished discipline, it also inhibits the choice that sociology can offer of ways of being interested in the social world. The subject has not yet reached the stage, if it ever will, where we can happily sit back in the sure and certain knowledge that its basic principles have been satisfactorily established and disagreement over fundamentals laid to rest.

Sociology may not have any fundamental principles to speak of, but these are not to be had for the asking and by prematurely closing off areas of dispute. Fundamentals, if we are to have them, are hard won and take years of patient thought and effort, by confronting problems squarely, working at their solution, opting for theoretical and empirical strategies to see where they might lead, and so on. Fundamentals are not to be had by pretending that one point of view, one approach, has all the answers. It might indeed turn out to have all the answers, though this is highly improbable, but this is something which needs to be shown in argument, debate, resolving problems, and in fruitful research: in general, by demonstrating its investigative power.

So, in this guide to sociology we emphasise the argumentative nature of the discipline above all else: a justification which will appear, in various ways, throughout the book. It is a view of the discipline which is, we admit, at odds with the normal conception of sociology. We make no apology for this: on the contrary. For us, one of the enticing and attractive features of sociology is that, potentially, it offers a wide range of ways of being interested in social life. It is very much open, full of problems, debates, provocative ideas, and intellectual challenges, as we have said earlier. In which case, at the present state of affairs, we think it as important to 'play with ideas', be outrageous even, as it is to be concerned with producing facts or true theories about society and social life (both of which are matters we shall address later in the book). If this is all sociology is to aim for nothing could be easier. Producing facts about social life is not difficult: as ordinary mortals going about our daily life we do this all the time. What is more difficult, as we shall try to show, is producing good *sociological* ideas about social life, just as it is difficult to produce good ideas in physics, in biology, in linguistics, in psychology, in economics, and so on. Accordingly, though this guide to sociology is unorthodox we find this no bad thing. Whether it works or not is, of course, another matter.

Moreover, we admit that the qualities we find in sociology may not suit everyone. We do not think that sociology is some wonderful experience to be had by every right-thinking gentleman or gentlewoman. People have a perfect right to be uninterested in it, just as those who are interested in sociology have a perfect right to quarrel with our way of presenting the subject. Our aim is not to close off argument but to open it. Moreover, we try to do this in as non-partisan a way as possible. Although we shall have critical things to say, we intend these to be fair-minded, not aimed at purveying our own sociological inclinations. The problems and difficulties we identify we want to treat as every sociologist's problems and difficulties. Problems are everywhere, in every approach, in every perspective, and in this sense we are all in the same boat.

How should this book be used? In no sense is it intended to provide a comprehensive coverage of all the major theories, areas, and significant findings in sociology. There are a number of excellent texts which do this. Instead what we aim to offer is a guide to sociological reasoning, to some of the ways to respond to the argumentative nature of the subject. It is, as we say, a guide not a directory, and in this sense complements other more comprehensive texts and, further, presumes some familiarity with the discipline. As teachers of sociology of long standing, we have tried to respond to some of the bewilderments our students have expressed over the years about sociology, not necessarily to suggest that the confusions are unfounded (many of them are manifestly not), but trying to show how a reasoned approach to them can be made. Each chapter deals with a number of issues germane to current debates within sociology and which, also, are the source of much confusion, for beginners especially. In the first we introduce a metaphorical device, sociology as a collection of games, for looking at sociology which we think rather more useful than the perspectival one currently used widely. This is followed by three chapters which deal, in various ways, with some vexing matters to do with theories and theorising, including the relationship between sociology and philosophy, the argument nature of the subject, the persistence of alternative sociological approaches, and choosing options in theorising. The remaining chapters are rather more self-contained, treating topics such as the scientific status of sociology and what might be involved in achieving it, methods and empirical research, and, finally, how to go about the business of reading sociology using the example of Goffman's work: all of which constitute areas of misunderstanding and confusion for beginners and, dare we add, for those longer in the sociological tooth.

Finally, we have not followed the usual practice of footnoting. Much of what follows is difficult enough without overburdening the audience further. Instead, after each chapter we append a short section on sources and further reading.

Chapter 1
AN ANALOGY FOR SOCIOLOGY: PERSPECTIVES VERSUS A COLLECTION OF GAMES

In their first encounter with sociology many students, and by no means the poorer ones, display more than just a little puzzlement about the way in which sociologists seem to go about their business. This provokes a litany of familiar complaints: the subject is too theoretical, too factual, states the obvious in obscure jargon, does not seem to go anywhere, never seems to resolve anything but meanders around aimlessly, and more. The usual response of teachers is to pretend that all these complaints are, at bottom, ill-founded, or characteristic of a young discipline, or testimony to the great difficulties involved in making the subject into a proper science, or some such. But, whatever the truth of these defences, the point is that in the end they amount to excuses that sociology is not more like other disciplines, that it fails to meet the aspirations of a bone fide science, fails to provide the key to the good life, or lacks the foundations of an adequate intellectual discipline. In short, that it fails to live up to its advertising. Once again, there is some truth in all of these views. Sociology is often pictured as a discipline at constant war with itself with Conflict Theorists attacking Functionalists, Structuralists skirmishing with Interpretativists, Interactionists ambushing Positivists, and Marxists taking on all comers. Although a rather overblown image, sociology as civil war does at least capture the almost incessant manner in which the discipline, no doubt to the puzzlement and amusement of well-established social sciences, questions and argues about practically everything. Indeed, the currently popular way of presenting sociology as a collection of perspectives recognises that the discipline has failed to produce a set of coherent principles capable of building a cumulative and integrated body of knowledge. It can only achieve, that is, angles of vision on the social world.

Sociology is riddled with disagreements. There are different points of view, often fundamental ones, at almost every level. This is a basic fact about the discipline which needs to be faced squarely, not excused or fudged. Only in this way can the important issues and difficulties be handled with the care and attention they deserve. In other words, it is our view that the complaints and excuses concerning the discipline we indicated earlier are not so much wrong but misdirect our attention and effort from trying to understand just what the difficulties are, how they may be faced, and where they might lead sociological inquiries. No intellectual pursuit worth the name is without disagreements: these are its life-blood. And it is our purpose in this book to explore some of the salient disagreements in sociology, showing what is involved in the arguments for various positions. We do not propose to do this by suggesting that we will resolve the arguments: it is not that easy and nor should we expect it to be so. Our purpose is well served if we are able to illuminate what the arguments and the difficulties are about. The effort to do this is what the rest of the book is about.

This chapter begins that effort by building upon some criticisms of a common device for organising the mass of sociological theories and ideas, not only for beginners but also for those who have been in the discipline for some time, namely, sociology as a set of perspectives. In what follows we express some doubts about this metaphor, not because it is a metaphor, but because it is an inappropriate and less than useful one which closes off the opportunity for proper socio-logical argument, mainly by encouraging the global condemnation of bodies of sociological ideas without much detailed thought and exami-nation. During the course of the discussion we shall also introduce an alternative metaphor for thinking about sociology, namely, sociology as a collection of games. Rather than state in advance what this metaphor is intended to do, we prefer to let this emerge during the discussion where, or so we hope, its point can be more clearly appre-ciated by giving it work to do in our argument. There is, however, one warning we wish to give at the outset. Picturing sociology as a collec-tion of games is intended as a metaphor: a way of clarifying something which is vague, too complex for easy apprehension, or only dimly perceived by means of an example from a more familiar domain. We are not, in other words, saying that sociology *is* a game, though many hardened professionals might cynically concur that it is. Our aim is to bring some features of games into an analogous relationship with sociology in order to illuminate aspects, qualities, or connections we think important. The metaphor is a visual device for looking at the discipline and its practices. We do, of course, recognise that meta-phors can be dangerous things: indeed, this is the burden of our complaint against the perspectives metaphor in that it misleads more than it clarifies. Neverthless, despite this risk, we offer the game metaphor as a resource for thinking about sociology and its problems. Once it has done its job it can, and ought to be, discarded.

The following discussion is organised as follows: first, we shall look at the notion that sociology can be summarised as a set of perspectives; second, we will elaborate our reservations about this idea by reviewing the way in which it predisposes certain kinds of critical appraisal; third, we will examine our alternative idea, sociology as a collection of games; finally, we will discuss some of the characteristics our way of picturing sociology brings to the fore.

SOME VIRTUES AND VICES OF THE PERSPECTIVAL APPROACH

A currently popular way of introducing the main ideas of sociology is to present the discipline as a set of perspectives. A perspective ('paradigm', 'approach', and 'theory' are terms also used) is a collection of ideas and methods which constitute a more or less unified approach to the conceptualisation of some or all of sociology's subject-matter. Thus, students are presented with Marxist, Functionalist, and Interactionist approaches, to mention but one widely used and familiar way of describing sociology's perspectives. Each of these labels refers to, and collects together, ideas, theories, methods, arguments, scholars, sociological works, findings, as typical ways of posing and dealing with sociology's topics. As a simplifying device orienting the beginner to a discipline which lacks an overall structure, it can be as helpful as any as a way of organising sociology.

There is, however, an important ambiguity involved in the idea of perspectives. The expression itself, taken from painting, suggests 'points of view' taken with respect to the same subject-matter. In other words, the relationship between 'points of view' is a complementary one, each linked to the others by the fact that they are about the same subject. Different perspectives bring different aspects of an object into view and though the things they show look different, they are complementary, not competitive. They are different angles on the same thing. Taken together they give a more rounded picture of the whole than does any one of them on its own. Thus, on this interpretation of the perspective's metaphor, sociology as a discipline based around perspectives consists of a variety of ways of looking at sociological things, each of which yields its distinctive but legitimate portrayal of society and social life.

There is, however, another way of looking at the various perspectives, not as a series of views on sociology's subject-matter, not as a set of complementary accounts of social life, but as a variety of attitudes towards the nature of sociology itself in which the very idea of sociology's subject-matter is in dispute. On this interpretation, perspectives are not complementary but competitive. Each seeks to present a comprehensive and self-sufficient conception of what sociology might be. They do not show different aspects of the same thing, but make very different claims as to what the thing is; they compete, so to speak, for the same space.

Perspectives, then, can be treated in one of two ways: ways not always clearly distinguished. First, as embodiments of differential emphases which are complementary in the sense that one is a corrective to another. An example of this is the claim that macrosociological theories should be underpinned by a corresponding concern for the individual and the microsociological. Or, in terms of the perspectives we identified earlier, the view that Functionalist theory, or its descendants, with their emphasis on the systemic interconnections between the elements of the social system, could be reconciled with, or added to, the Marxian emphasis on societally generated conflict and change. Such arguments call for a synthesis of two or more points of view. Each contains, as it were, a germ of the truth and one of the theoretical tasks of sociology is to synthesise or reconcile them to obtain a fuller, a truer, a more rounded account of society and social life. Second, perspectives can be treated as antithetical to one another. The life of the discipline is a struggle between them until one is left in sole possession of the field. The relationship between perspectives is one of conflict, each one aiming to occupy the whole territory of sociology by showing that there is no sociological problem which cannot be brought under the aegis of the favoured way of looking at things. The validity of other points of view is to be questioned until they cede the ground. So, what we have here is not so much reconciliation of different points of view through argument and synthesis, but each perspective seeking hegemony over the rest.

One of the virtues of the perspectival approach to organising sociological ideas is that it recognises the variety in sociological work, but does so by committing the vice of oversimplifying some differences within the discipline at the expense of others. Of course, like any classification, dividing the subject up into perspectives will only serve the purpose, well or badly, for which it is designed. Different designs using different criteria to create the classification would produce different perspectival collections. However, our major concern is that perspectives become ossified as the only way of looking at sociology, so shaping the discussion and argument in the discipline as if the major problems are about synthesising the various theoretical approaches or demonstrating that one is manifestly superior to the others. As a way of reflecting the variety of sociological work, classifying the corpus into a collection of perspectives can only succeed by 'fudging' important and interesting differences in the interests of typological symmetry. If the perspectival device is recognised as an educational convenience, a place from which to begin, then it has few, if any, damaging effects and, in fact, positive virtues. Unfortunately, however, some perspectives have crystallised into institutions invoked by both students and professionals as ways of locating and discussing instances of sociological work, thereby preventing understanding of the work in its own terms. Perspectives tend to be rationalisations of a body of knowledge and, in this sense, oversimplify by encouraging the notion they are relatively fixed and immutable sets of ideas, their core principles remaining unchanged. This is, to say the least, a misleading picture of the way in which ideas change, are modified, resurface through time. What constituted the 'essence' of Marxism in the late nineteenth century was very different from that of fifty years later and different still from that of today. Similarly, Interactionism and Functionalism, to mention but two more perspectives in sociology, display the same qualities of change and modification.

Of course, perspectives need not end up as frozen atemporal encapsulations of ideas. They could retain their vigour, recognising their own changing quality, except that the force of the metaphor, the notion of perspective, would begin to lose some of its sharpness. Be this as it may, irrespective of whether perspectives are seen as complementary emphases or as combatants fighting for the ground of sociology, one task they do set for the beginning student is that, somehow, he or she has to make a judgement, a choice, about which is the more promising, the more plausible, the more correct, and so on. Whatever else they may be, perspectives are about different ways of looking at the social world through sociological eyes, which means that they are involved in an argument with one another, whether this be for synthesis or for execution. Of course, such a choice cannot be made without some study, looking at research done under the auspices of the particular perspectives, closely examining the cogency, the coherence of the ideas, and so on, followed by a careful weighing of the respective merits and demerits of each. However, one virtue of the perspectival device is its economic packaging of what are, in detail, complex chains of argument, but which can so easily turn into the vice of summary dismissal without serious attention. To see what can be involved here, we want to examine one way in which perspectives are often contrasted, using as an example what is a fairly familiar critique of Functionalism. Let us hasten to add that we are not suggesting that Functionalism is right, or wrong for that matter; we use it mainly because these days it receives less attention than it deserves. Our purpose is to illustrate what sociological argument should *not* be about and the case of Functionalism serves this purpose more than adequately.

THE ARGUMENT OVER FUNCTIONALISM

In comparing anything a common standard on which to ground the comparison is necessary. In the case of sociological perspectives one such standard could be the extent to which the perspectives being compared are right about, to put it crudely, the way things are in society. Although perspectives will say different things about society, may even contradict each other, one is to prefer that which makes the most sense and which is right, or more nearly right, about the way things are. So, a possible criticism against a perspective is that it disregards obvious and indisputable facts about the social world. It is in this respect that Functionalism is often charged with denying the historical nature of social phenomena, something which Marxism, for example, insists upon. The charge can go further, and does, by accusing Functionalism of ideological perversion of the facts by denying the possibility of social change, so giving the present society an aura of permanency and immutability, discouraging efforts to change it. Worse, Functionalism is also charged with portraying society as a harmony of interests, as a self-regulating system which is all for the best in the best of all possible worlds.

All of this is normally enough to secure a conviction without further ado. Society obviously is a historical phenomenon. Previous societies have come into being and passed out of existence just as ours will. Our own society is in an ongoing process of change, as is only too visible to anyone not wholly blinded by prejudice or beguiled by enticing harmonious pictures of society. Functionalism is in error because it blandly denies what is more or less a matter of obvious fact. It fails to match up to the test of telling us how society really is. We might want to say here, and this is where the notion of 'game' begins to have a use, that the critics score over the Functionalists, say, for the sake of argument, have a 3–0 lead over them.

Although putting the matter this way no doubt seems a little artful, it does, none the less, allow us to talk about some of the real difficulties involved in comparing perspectives. To pursue the analogy further: to say that a score is 3–0 is, in fact, to say very little unless we know what game is being played. If the game is soccer it is one thing, but its significance is something else again if the game is snooker. Even in soccer, while 3–0 is a comfortable lead, it can be reversed unless, of course, it is a final score. In other words, knowing what a score signifies depends a great deal upon the game being played. Similarly, the effectiveness of a criticism, an objection, depends a great deal on the nature of the intellectual 'game' being played, of the ways in which what is said comprises moves within these 'games', how 'points' are awarded, and how they total up to give decisive outcomes, if they do. So, in the case of the attack on Functionalism, in order to see how decisive the arguments are, we need to look closely at Functionalism itself: to examine, that is, how this 'game' is actually played. We need to see what Functionalism itself says, what it proposes as a way of conceptualising society, not a version of Functionalism put forward by what could be the myopic eyes of some alternative perspective.

The charge is that Functionalism is ahistorical and, thereby, unable to explain social change. But, if we refer to one of the important founders of modern Functionalism, Emile Durkheim, then even a superficial perusal of his works will show that they are deeply influenced by historical considerations. In his *Rules of Sociological Method* he stresses that functions in society can only be identified by comparing societies at the same stages of development. In his *Division of Labour in Society* he seeks to examine the changing function of law in the context of a massive historical shift from the traditional to a more modern type of society. He also chooses to study aboriginal totemism as a key to the understanding of the function of religion in evolutionary terms. And, by way of final example, his *Socialism* seeks to show that socialism is a consequence of historical development of the increasing predominance of the economy in the organisation of society. So, as far as Durkheim is concerned, there is no suggestion that Functionalism is antithetical to historical understanding.

Nor need any suggestion be made about his followers. While many of them did reject historical explanation this was specifically directed against those forms of historical explanation which consisted, in the main, of speculative evolutionary explanations largely devoid of evidence to support them. Against a policy of treating institutions as mere survivals left over from an earlier period of history, such as religion, the Functionalist heuristic of looking to what contemporary role an institution might play in society is wholly reasonable. It does not require a rejection of history and change, only the separation of two kinds of questions which may be independent of each other: what brings an institution into being and, once it exists, what sustains it? Thus, Gregory Bateson, in introducing his Functionalist account of ceremonies in Iatmul Culture, writes,

> It is of course true that the ceremonies have had a history and it would no doubt be possible to speculate about that history. But that is not my purpose. I shall be content only to show some of the sorts of functional relationship which exist between the ceremonies and the remainder of the contemporary culture of the Iatural. Perhaps, in the future, a clearer understanding of the synchronic aspects of society will enable us to isolate and define the diachronic, the processes of cultural change.

Functionalism, then, does not oppose historical explanation but does require for its rational interpretation, some recognition of 'explanatory relativity', a notion we deal with in more detail in Chapter 2, namely, the realisation that not everything is to be explained in the same way, that not everything is to be given a historical explanation any more than everything requires a functional one.

What about the charge that Functionalism is ideologically motivated in suggesting the undesirability and impossibility of change by portraying society as a harmony of stabilised and beneficial arrangements? Talcott Parsons, the key figure in modern Functionalism, is often accused of this despite the fact that his work shows that he is well aware of change and disharmony in society. He identifies two kinds of changes: those that take place within the system (analogous to the changing composition of cells within the organism), changes which do not transform the whole into something new; and changes of the system in which the nature of the system as a whole is altered. Even a system in 'equilibrium' is not unchanging as, for example, the human organism though in 'equilibrium' develops from baby to infant to child to adolescent to adult.

As far as the harmony of interests is concerned, Parsons often used the idea of the perfectly integrated system but, as he repeatedly emphasised, only for theoretical purposes. He claimed that this usage was equivalent to the physicist's use of the idea of the 'frictionless machine'. No scientist supposes that such a machine is empirically possible though it is a useful idea to think with, draw out causal relations, identify variables, and so on. It is a simplification and idealisation. Parsons does not suggest that society is harmonious, for empirical cases cannot approach this theoretically limiting idea. Even under the most favourable conditions for social harmony, the sociological equivalent of entropy, the tendency towards disorder, would produce some disorganisation. If nothing else did, sheer randomness would produce disharmony. In the real world there will be greater or lesser degrees of 'structural strain', of disintegration, built into the social system: a product of the organisation of the system itself.

In sum, a great deal of the attack on Functionalism misses the point by failing to appreciate the 'game' the Functionalists are playing. Their aim was to explore the consequences of the idea of 'system' in the study of societies, so developing a mode of analysis which dealt with questions about social organisation independent of, not opposed to, historical inquiries. For anthropology, where much of Functionalism was developed, this mode of analysis was particularly useful in studying preliterate societies where historical data were unavailable. As a theoretical strategy it scheduled sociological tasks by proposing that problems of 'synchronic', or contemporary, analysis, be taken before those of 'diachronic', or change, analysis, as a way of identifying base lines against which changes could be precisely measured.

There is much more that could be said about this debate. For immediate purposes, however, the point we are making is, to repeat, not that Functionalism is right, or wrong, but that it is a more limited doctrine than it is often taken to be. Nor is it so rashly contrary to fact as is often made out. If one asks about the part the ideas of 'function', 'harmony', 'stability', and the rest, play within the Functionalist 'game', then perhaps one may begin to see what kind of ideas they are.

There are a number of lessons, or so we hope, to be learned from this debate. We have no quarrel with the criteria selected for evaluating a perspective, namely, whether or not it accurately portrays how things are in society, to put it simply, only that it is not as straightforward a criterion as it looks. But more on this later. Our main point is that a detailed look at what those labelled, and may be criticised for, as belonging to a perspective say often reveals them to be far from deluded fools but people making determined efforts to say something of sociological value. What they say may, in the end, turn out to wrong, but rarely is it unreasoned. Further, it should also show that in trying to understand what is being said there is no short cut, no handy formula, such as a perspectival label, which does not, thereby, distort or misrepresent the reasoned effort the ideas represent.

So far we have made one use of the game analogy to indicate some of the issues involved in comparing perspectives. From now on we want to develop it further, once again in connection with the task of coming to terms with the different approaches to be found within the discipline.

THE DIVERSITY OF GAMES

One notable feature of games is their diversity. Thus, 'football' names a collection of games which includes soccer, Rugby, both League and Union, American football, the Eton wall game, and others. 'Cards' denotes a collection which includes, among others, canasta, whist, bridge, poker, happy families, while 'board games' includes chess, draughts, ludo, and so on. Here what we have is not just a diversity of types of game, but a diversity within the types themselves. In which case it becomes difficult to see quite what it is the members of each collection share, let alone what it is that makes them games. The diversity, so to speak, overwhelms us. However, just because we can recognisably and sensibly collect together a set of games under, for example, the label 'football' it does not follow that the games share any one thing in common; some one quality which makes them a member of this collection rather than another. In fact, as the diversity should indicate, there are all kinds of connections that might be drawn between games, some historical, some in terms of the skills required, some because they are played by teams, some because they share similar aims, and more. And it is in this way that we want to think of sociology as a collection of games. What unites the particular games, if anything, what connections may be drawn between them, is a matter of inquiry and argument not presumption. All of which implies that comparing games is no straightforward affair. Are football games better than board games? Are card games better than both of these? Within the collection 'football' is Rugby League better than Rugby Union? And so on. Without specifying the respects in which games are to be compared such questions are not only difficult to answer but hard to comprehend. What is more, it makes little sense to suppose that all games can be compared with one another and ranked on some absolute scale of relative superiority. And so it is, we want to say, with sociology 'games'.

We must be careful and clear about what is being said here. We are not suggesting that sociology 'games', to use our metaphor, cannot be compared and that, in the end, it is all a matter of opinion. We are saying that it makes no sense to suppose that they can all be compared and all ranked on a single scale of superiority. This is far from saying that they cannot be compared. One can find, say, that Rugby League is not as rough as Rugby Union, that card games are not so demanding in physical prowess as ball games, that other games are not so popular as association football, and so on. In other words, games can be compared in given respects. Our point is not that games cannot be compared but that the problems arise because there are so many ways of comparing them, and so many combinations in which they can be compared. The problem is not that we are prevented from making this or that comparison, but that the comparisons cannot be aggregated into a single scalar comparison which will give a verdict that, say, soccer is the best game, baseball next, golf third, and so on.

The same goes for sociology 'games'. We certainly do not want to say that comparisons of them cannot be made, but we do want to maintain that aggregate judgements of their relative merits are complex and, as we hope to have indicated in our discussion of Functionalism, a tricky business to suggest that one 'game' is better than others, or worse, *tout court*. Certainly preferences can be formed in terms of what can be got out of a particular sociology 'game'. One may, for the sake of argument, opt for Marxism on the grounds that it provides a more direct recognition of the role of class and class conflict in modern society than does Functionalism. If this is what is required then it is a good basis for a preference. If, however, one wishes to direct attention to the internal structure of a sysem of social relations, then, arguably, this is something Functionalism provides better than Marxism.

This does not mean that the choice of perspective, theory, approach, or, in our terms, 'game' comes down to preferences alone. It does serve to show another difficulty in the way of straightforward comparisons of sociology 'games', namely, that they have different 'problems' or, in recent jargon, 'problematics'. Different games have different objectives. In chess the aim is to checkmate the opponent's king, in soccer to score more goals, in racing to be first past the post and, in the same way, different sociology 'games' have different aims or objectives. Since we shall be laying great stress on the problem-oriented nature of sociological reasoning in much of what follows, it is worth looking at this in some detail.

One of the more seductive temptations in comparing the different approaches to sociology is to treat them all as if they were addressed to the same problem and, accordingly, can be assessed in terms of their respective success in solving it. Admittedly there is a broad sense in which it could be said that all sociology 'games' share the same problem. Just as a large number of games provide fun for the players, so sociology 'games' could be said to share the aim of providing an effective framework for sociological analysis, even a scientific sociology. Unfortunately, such a goal is so diffuse that one of the first problems that any sociology will have to face is deciding what to mean by an 'effective framework' or a 'scientific sociology'. Some approaches will give priority to conforming to what are held to be the requirements of scientific procedure, while others may concentrate their attention on delineating the phenomena sociology will have to examine. Both, in their different ways, pursue the same objective but take very different routes. So, although sociologies might be said to share the same objective, they are apt to have different ideas as to what sociological problems need to be solved in the pursuit of that goal. In detail, then, sociology 'games' are not trying to solve the same problems, and attempts to treat them as if they were can lead to serious misunderstandings. What kind of misunderstandings can be illustrated by the example of another fairly familiar argument over 'Structuralist' and 'Interactionist' sociologies.

The distinction between Structuralist and Interactionist approaches is often construed as one of relative emphasis. The Structuralists seek to analyse society as a whole by trying to treat social phenomena as derivatives of social systemic properties. Marxists and Functionalists would both fall into this category. Interactionists, on the other hand, emphasise the importance of studying face-to-face interaction without reference to the system in which it may be implicated. Symbolic Interactionists and Ethnomethodologists would fit here. However, treating the matter in this way can lead to two important mistakes: first, making misplaced criticisms and, second, conveying a misleading impression of complementarity. For example, Interactionism is often criticised for its inability to answer questions that Structuralists want to answer. What is required, or so it is implied, is a synthesis of the two approaches; in effect, that the Interactionist account of social organisation needs contexting within an account of the system as a whole.

However, this criticism, and its proposed solution, misses the point that most Interreactionist approaches are not trying to answer the kind of questions Structuralists want to ask. In other words, they are not failing to answer Structuralist questions since they were never asked. In the same way, the idea that Interactionism complements Structural analysis, that the two can be synthesised, often involves a failure to appreciate that concentration on one kind of question obscures the sight of another one. Paying attention to Structuralist problems simply excludes attention to those that Interactionists want to address, and vice versa. We do not criticise soccer because it does not teach us how to score runs.

The point here can be illustrated by a brief look at the relationship between Ethnomethodology and other sociological approaches, what it calls 'constructivist sociologies'. Ethnomethodology argues that within the frameworks of such sociologies it is impossible to ask the questions Ethnomethodology wants to examine. That is, Ethnomethodology is incompatible with 'constructivist sociologies' because it poses problems for which there is no room in these other sociologies. They presuppose the resolution of the very things Ethnomethodology want to make problematic, two interests which cannot be sustained at the same time. Take the activity of asking and answering questions. Much sociological research involves asking people questions and using their replies as data for understanding social organisation. Using the answers, to put it another way, as indicative of attitudes, beliefs, statements about social relationships, and so on. The interview is a classic example of this. From Ethnomethodology's point of view, however, this technique presupposes that the members of society share a common language and have mutual understanding so that the questions put to them are understood in much the same way by all respondents, and their answers similarly equivalent in meaning. Ethnomethodology, on the other hand, seeks to raise the question of how mutual understanding and sense is itself achieved and organised. How, for example, is the asking and answering of questions organised by the parties to an encounter? In other words, it is not so much a matter here of different ways of looking at the same thing, but with ways of looking at different things: the question-answer exchange as a method of finding out about people's beliefs, attitudes, and so on, and with a speech exchange system as a communication arrangement. Both of these interests cannot be sustained at the same time.

In more general terms, then, emphasising the objectives of an approach allows us to abandon the 'whole story' treatment of sociological approaches, both in respect of assuming that any approach bids to provide the whole story for sociology and that the different approaches, taken collectively, add up to a unified theory. An approach is not incomplete because it does not answer the questions that other approaches pose, any more than soccer is incomplete because it does not allow the player to carry the ball in the way Rugby does.

Again we must be careful about what is being said here. In saying, as we do, that the different sociology 'games' do not add up, so to speak, is not to say that they are not worth playing. Nor is it to go so far as to suggest that they never could add up and that sociology is doomed to remain an assemblage of discrepant ways of investigating social life. These are matters for the future. There is, however, one lesson we can draw from the discussion so far and this is that approaches need to be judged in terms of how well they answer their own problems. Just because an approach is directed towards a problem does not, of course, ensure that even by its own standards it provides a satisfactory solution: a matter complicated by the fact that approaches do not usually have one problem, though they may have a 'master' one. Attempts to solve 'subsidiary' problems can have all kinds of repercussions within the overall framework.

So far we have used the game metaphor to illuminate some of the difficulties involved in comparing sociological approaches. But, in pointing to such difficulties, we do not want to imply that, in the end, selecting a perspective is really just a matter of opinion. As we have already said, the choice of perspective or approach is influenced by, among other things, the kinds of problems or puzzles one wishes to address. But, the matter does not end there for the way in which the problem is to be addressed is also a methodical not an opinionated business. And, to illustrate this, we want to make use of another characteristic of games, one which gives them their point, namely, that they are played within constraints.

THE CONSTRAINED NATURE OF GAMES

Games are played according to rules, and using this idea we want to point to some of the constraints that sociologists observe when they 'play with ideas'. Although many of the rules governing games are vague, even made up as one goes along as in many children's games, without the quality of constraint that rules provide, games would cease to be recognisable as games. Although we commonly think of rules as devices designed to prevent us doing something, be it smoking, walking on the grass, taking a car without the owner's permission, and so forth, this is not their only aspect. In games, for example, rules not only forbid us to do certain things otherwise we are penalised, they also tell us *how* to play the game. Without the rules of chess defining the pieces, the board, the legitimate moves each piece can make, what constitutes winning and losing, and so on, all we have is pieces of wood or moulded plastic and a checkered board. We could no more imagine playing chess without its rules than we could imagine playing soccer using the rules of cricket. The rules are, in this sense, enabling: they tell us what the game is about and how it is to be distinguished from other games.

We have to recognise that games exhibit no little variety in the formality, the precision, and the clarity of their rules. Games such as chess, hockey, soccer, Rugby, and many more, which have long-established traditions and are organised by some controlling authority, have widely agreed and written rules which, within appropriate circumstances, are publicly enforceable. Children's games, on the other hand, if they do not almost entirely consist in arguments about rules, have more informal, *ad hoc* rules. However, this variety need not impede us. All we need to accept is that games just do show, among other things, variety in the precision, formality, and clarity of their rules. And so we should expect with sociology 'games'.

There is another feature we need to emphasise here. Game rules, like all rules, have to be applied in situations, on occasions, with respect to particular players and their actions. It is this contextual aspect which gives rules their life. Which means that it is always a matter of judgement and, as every soccer player knows, argument as to whether or not the rules have been applied correctly. Further, knowing all the rules of a game, say, knowing all the rules and regulations contained in the *Football Association Handbook,* or knowing all the allowable moves in chess, will not turn anyone into a player. Knowing all the rules will not tell us how to develop attacking moves, how to use space, draw opponents out of position, and so on: all the skills necessary to be a good, in this example, footballer. Games, that is, can be played well or badly, expertly or inexpertly.

The rules of games, then, give the conditions of legitimate play. They specify what moves can and cannot be made in playing the game. The rules are impersonal in that they govern the activities of all players independently of their particular preferences. The whole point about games, we might say, is that they are erected as impersonal constructions using sets of rules which specify what it is to make a move within the game.

Let us now try to relate this discussion of games and their rules to sociology. We are now in a position to see an important contrast the game analogy makes with perspectivalism. Whereas the latter emphasises 'fields of view' or 'angles of vision' on the social world, the game metaphor emphasises what we might call the 'practices' used in the playing of sociology 'games'. Practices which can be seen in the activities which produce the corpus of materials, ideas, findings, and so on, that constitute the discipline at any point in time. It is to begin to emphasise sociology not as a set of facts, findings, or even as a body of knowledge, though all of these are features of the subject, but as a set of practices sociologists use when playing their 'games'. In this sense, sociology 'games' consist in sets of activities more or less skilfully put together. As soccer consists in, but is not exhausted by, the use of various skills such as dribbling, kicking the ball, using space, using pace, tackling, drawing opponents out of position, and so on, so we can conceive of sociology 'games' as assembled out of appropriate activites such as theorising, using evidence, producing data, presenting an argument, all within rule-like constraints which 'players' must interpret as best they can.

In later chapters we will discuss in further detail some of the activities and skills used in the playing of sociology 'games'. For now we want to elaborate the conception we have just sketched.

THE SELF-SUFFICIENCY OF GAMES

Earlier when discussing some of the difficulties involved in comparing different approaches in sociology, we made use of a tempting standard that might be employed in choosing between them, namely, the extent to which they accord with reality. It is a tempting standard because sociology set itself up to be an empirical discipline. Indeed, this is a source of a number of difficulties students often find with sociology, for although it claims to be empirical or, to put it another way, put forward true statements about social life, it goes about this in a decidedly unstraightforward manner. And here we are making even heavier weather of the business by talking about game metaphors when what we should be doing is getting on with comparing approaches with reality. It would indeed be nice if matters were this simple. If all that mattered were saying true things about reality nothing could be easier. 'Bob Anderson is five foot eleven and lives in Derbyshire' and 'Wes Sharrock and John Hughes are overweight' are both true statements. They get the facts right. But this hardly gives them scientific, or even sociological, significance. There is much more to the saying of some things about the world than that they are merely true.

The notion of game may help us see what is at stake here. Games can usefully be regarded as ends in themselves. The interest they have lies in their playing despite what other aims we might want to achieve in addition, be they fitness, demonstrating our athletic prowess, sublimating hatred on the spouse, or whatever. Just as a natural scientist may practise science to further the welfare of humanity, save the world or destroy it, secure personal wealth, or just for the joy of it, these have nothing to do with how science is practised; nothing to do with how to play the game. So, we want to regard sociology 'games' as played for their own sake: you either want to play them or you do not. However, be this as it may, the self-sufficiency of games allows us to talk about the support sociological statements about the world need; that is, about the ideas concerning how they are to be understood, how they are to be seen as applying to the world, what kind of procedures will test out the ideas, and so on. Sociology 'game's' rules are not just designed to govern what they can say about the world, but also how they can produce the things they say and decide whether or not what is said is correct. The illusion is, as we have pointed out before, to think that although the different sociological approaches differ in what they say about the world all can be put together against a common standard for testing whether what they say is true or not. Approaches need to be compared in terms of their ideas about the 'truth conditions' appropriate for their work. For example, some Marxists, in dubbing their work 'dialectical' do so in a manner closely affiliated with Hegel's use of this term. This means that as far as they are concerned, the usual rules of logic do not apply since these are regarded as subordinate to those of dialectical logic. Hence, to be found, in terms of formal logic, contradicting oneself would be, for many, a decisive blow against an argument; for those governed by dialectical logic this would be anything but a telling criticism.

Although there are other issues here, many of which are quite difficult, a fuller treatment will have to wait its appointed place. Nevertheless, the general point we are making here is an important one. As far as intellectual activities are concerned, measuring statements against reality is no straightforward affair. If it were why has our science, taken by most as the yardstick of empirical knowledge, taken so many centuries to get where it has? However, as social beings ourselves it is perhaps hard to see what all the fuss is about as far as sociology is concerned. As social beings there is surely a strong sense in which we already know about the social world; after all, it is our world. Unfortunately, it does not follow from this that we know such a world *sociologically*.

SOCIOLOGICAL THEORISING

So far we have said little about what makes the collection of sociology 'games' sociology and not, say, economics, political science, biology, or even ordinary games like football or cricket. What is it that makes them a recognisable collection of sociology 'games' and not just a variegated set of unrelated activities? The ready, and no doubt unhelpful answer is that they are recognised as such by those in a position to know. And, of course, the 'games' themselves are often proposals about what is to constitute sociology: a right that we do not wish to usurp by proposing our own definition of the discipline. Nevertheless, despite our reluctance to engage in definitional stipulation, it is worth briefly discussing the root idea that informs the sociological enterprise.

The root notion of the discipline is that human actions are inter-connected in complicated, often imperfectly perceived ways. Many of the basic theoretical concepts of sociology, despite fundamental variations in their meaning, such as 'social structure', 'culture', 'group', 'institution', and others, embody, indeed formulate, the idea that human actions are situated in complexes of other actions and actors. Sociology takes this feature of human life as something that can be studied, investigated, and theorised about, as a significant domain not reducible to the interests of other disciplines. At this level, this idea is not a theory. Nor is it a finding in the sense that sometime someone suddenly discovered that human actions are social. We have always known this. It is knowledge which, though not sociological, is intimately connected with our experience of human life itself. What sociology has done is turn this quite ordinary experience into a proposal for an intellectual activity. It serves as a foundation for sociology because it represents an election, a choice made by the discipline, and embodied in it, to take a special interest in this aspect of the world as an investigable, analysable, researchable domain: as something about which we can have theoretical not just practical knowledge. Of course it is the task of particular sociology 'games' to trace through the consequences of this foundational idea, stating it in more precise and rigorous terms, formulating theories, using them to produce findings, and so on. But it is this presuppositon of the interconnectedness of human actions which provides the space for sociology to live and pursue its inquiries.

We have just said that sociology's interest in the world is a theoretic not a practical one; that is, one of its essential activities is that of theorising, and theories one of its major products. From our point of view, theorising is a playing with ideas exhibiting a stance of reflec-tiveness on the world. By contrast, a practical attitude on the world is very much that. To replace a flat tyre, cook a meal, play scrabble, carry on a conversation, for example, we do not need to theorise about them, reflect on them, in order to get them done. We just do them as part and parcel of the ordinary routine practices of daily living. Practical interests are governed by the fact that we take the world as it is on trust, without particular reflection, without special attention to questions about why it is like it is. Which is not to say that a practical interest, practical knowledge, is inferior to theoretical interest and knowledge. Far from it. Both are different ways of being interested in the world: interests governed by different constraints. Theorising, then, is a kind of standing back, an attitude of reflection, which is not to say that it cannot be directed towards some practical end. This is certainly one way in which theorising can be done. We can take a theoretic interest, for example, in the mechanics of tyre construction, the physics of cooking, ask questions about the nature of word games, examine the organisational structure of conversations, and so on. Or, as Marx did, seek the practical end of overthrowing capitalism. Similarly, many sociologists are interested in social problems such as poverty, inequality, crime, mental illness, and so on, and motivated by a desire to remedy such ills. None the less, as sociologists their work is directed towards achieving a theoretical understanding of such matters. As in the case of Marx, his work reflects a theoretic attitude to the end of overthrowing capitalism. Alternatively, theorising can be motived by no other desire than to gain theoretical knowledge of some phenomenon, seeking, to put it more colloquially, knowledge for knowledge's sake. In other words, theorising can be an ingredient of many different kinds of sociology 'games' and can itself take various forms, as we shall see in more detail in Chapter 4.

Some theorists want to produce theories which look like those of natural science in being deductively organised, logically rigorous, highly operational, and predictively powerful. Others, and these are only two examples, seek theories which are designed to 'sensitise' researchers towards investigable problems. In sociology, matters are complicated by the fact that the term 'theory' covers a number of constructions not always clearly distinguished or distinguishable, including 'perspective', 'paradigm', 'approaches', 'models', 'heuristics', 'explanations', and others. Nevertheless, despite the confusion that often surrounds these terms, they at least indicate the varied kinds of activities that can constitute sociological theorising. Some theorising, for example, is more philosophical than empirical in character. Some is more stipulative in tone, recommending ways in which we should be interested in the world sociologically, and some is more concerned to explain findings about the social world. However, what we need to note for now is not so much what the various theoretical activities may be called, simply that sociological theorising is highly varied.

We said earlier that the root notion of the interconnectedness of human actions provides the space for sociology 'games' to seek their particular aims and aspirations. How, to put it another way, they will seek to implement their theoretic interest in the social world. However, the 'games' seek these aims within some broad constraints that govern all sociology 'games'. Some, indeed most of them, are constraints belonging to intellectual activities in general. In the remainder of this chapter we want to say a little about the ground rules of the 'games' sociologists play: some canons which they claim govern their endeavours, bearing in mind, of course, that making a claim is no guarantee that the claim will be upheld. As we have said before, games can be played well or badly. The ground rules we want to identify especially are the following: empirical orientation and contingency, the requirement of clarity, consistency, and coherence, and the need for explicitness.

SOME SOCIOLOGY GROUND RULES

The vast majority of sociologists look upon themselves as attempting to say something about the world and, thus, having to satisfy some test assessing what they say against how things are in the world. That is, their theorising has to have an empirical orientation and, at some point, satisfy empirical criteria. This leads directly on to contingency which involves recognising a difference between what sociologists say about the world and how they are in fact. It is a requirement, to put it another way, that sociological statements be capable of being confuted by findings. It is this that gives their statements scientific interest above and beyond their being simply true. 'Either the middle class possess 70 per cent of the nation's wealth or they do not' is true but of no scientific interest. Statements of scientific interest are those which might be wrong but which also might be right as decided by some genuinely independent test.

Clarity, consistency, and coherence are qualities which give a work an intelligible unity, difficult though this is to achieve. They are qualities closely linked to another ground rule, namely, the requirement for explicitness. What this means is that arguments have to be spelt out to an extent unusual in everyday life; laying out all the steps as clearly as possible. It is a requirement which leaves everything open to critical inspection.

Most of the ground rules we have identified are to do with the organisation and presentation of an argument: using ideas systematically, clearly, coherently, relating them to other ideas in as rigorous a way as possible, judging their significance, responding to criticism, taking account of telling points, gauging relevances, and the rest. Argument is the life of any intellectual endeavour. It is not a casual option but an essential part of the commitment to be interested in the world in an intellectual way. Marx, for example, quite early in his life had the idea that the revolutionary impulse to smash capitalism could only come from the working class, and yet it took him forty or so years to show why. All this work, in other words, is an extended argument to support his original idea.

None of this is meant to deny a role for imagination. Quite the contrary. But playing games, no matter how imaginative and inventive one wants to be, is about playing within constraints, and one of these is the requirement to be explicit in the moves that are made, the arguments that are advanced. Nor is it a constraint merely for the sake of constraint. In elaborating a problem it is not always clear quite what is involved, just as it is not always known in advance what a particular move commits a player to until some time after it has been made. Also, finding out what went wrong, and where, can be as important as finding out what went right. For both these ends, clarity and the rest are vital in argument. Sociology 'games', like other games, are full of surprises: sometimes a promising line of inquiry fails, just as the best team does not always win, whereas a not very serious idea might prove immensely fruitful. But to see why and how, the argument must be clearly arrayed.

When we introduced the topic of rules we noted that they are self-imposed constraints. And so it is with the ground rules we have just sketched. There is nothing to force us to obey them. After all, we do not have to take up chess, and there is nothing which can make us move the pieces according to the rules of the game. But, if we do not respect the rules much of the point of playing is lost. It is not the object of chess to place a piece so that it checkmates the opponent's king: it is, rather, to achieve this by obeying the rules. Similarly, though the ground rules for sociology are not as clear, perhaps, or as determinate as those of chess, the same point applies. This is why the object of sociology 'games' is not simply to say true things about the world, but to do so by clear argument not assertion, making the steps of the argument and evidence public and not concealing them from critical scrutiny, testing ideas genuinely, not fudging or, worse, cheating, and so on.

The game idea also allows us to see sociological ideas, theories, approaches not so much as pictures of the social world, but as instructions to other sociologists on how to produce such pictures; as rules for how to describe, analyse, and investigate society and social life sociologically. Just as, for an observer, perspective in painting makes scenes more realistic by showing objects in proportionate size to their distance from the viewer, so for the painter perspective is a way of geometrically organising the layout of a painting. In short, perspective in painting is a 'game' with rules, and it is in this sense that sociological approaches and theories are games with rules specifying what it is to know something sociologically.

One immediate complaint about what we have said so far, there are no doubt others, is that we have not distinguished sociology from other disciplines which deal with social life, or even from other activities which are concerned with human life but make no claims to scientific status, such as literature. This demarcation issue is certainly one which bothers many students. However, it is our view that territorial demarcations of this kind are not straightforward nor always clear. It is relatively easy to produce general descriptions of the differences, say, between sociology and psychology, on the lines that the former is concerned with collective life while the latter deals with individuals. As rough and ready orienting suggestions they are fair enough, but it takes little scrutiny to see that, in effect, they say very little. Sociology and psychology, to stick to our two examples, are different but, as with sociological perspectives, such differences are manifold, varied, and changing. There are considerable areas of overlap or, as sometimes regarded, disputed terrain between the two, and other disciplines, and no amount of effort to draw firm lines will ensure that they remain fixed. Disciplinary regions shade into one another and from any particular point it is not always easy to see if and where a border has been crossed. So it is with natural science. Working through ideas, trying to solve problems, seeing where an argument, a theory, might lead means that disciplines are always likely to run up against territory claimed by some other. What we should not do is confuse the organisation of disciplines, as exemplified in institutions such as universities, with the distinctive attitude a discipline reflects. And, of course, in the end what counts is what is being done, not necessarily what it is called.

The distinctiveness of interest a discipline exemplifies is, to use our metaphor, spelt out in the 'games' that make it up: games which may, of course, be closely related in some ways to those of other disciplines. The problems and issues bound up with the interrelationship between disciplines surface in a variety of ways that are impossible to encompass with a general definition of the relationship. In Chapter 2, for example, we discuss some facets of the relationship between sociology and philosophy and in Chapter 5 one way of effecting a connection between sociology and psychology. In both cases the issues we address are not simply about gross differences between two disciplines but concern other, and more important, matters. Like the notion of perspective, thinking about collections of ideas as 'disciplines' often gives the misleading impression that what we have before us are clearly demarcated, fixed collections of theories and findings organised around some core interest. This is not the case.

Thinking about games in this connection might help. Football and Rugby are different games. But what connections, what differences, are there between them? Both are played by teams, using balls, with the intention of scoring more than the opposing team. There may also be similarities in strategy and tactics. There are also differences. The balls are of different shape, the teams of different numbers, the rules different, and so on. In other words, while we accept that football and Rugby are different games, there may be all kinds of ways we can draw connections between them with – and this is important – particular purposes in mind, some which might require us to emphasise similarities, some their differences. What we do not have to do is worry overmuch about whether there is some single general principle which will demarcate one from another. And this is one way we think it useful to regard the differences between disciplines.

The above elements are the ones we want to emphasise from the 'game metaphor'. We do not pretend that all the characteristics of games are relevant to thinking about sociology. We could, for example, have suggested that games are intended as fun. We play games for amusement and entertainment, spend our leisure time enjoying them, and so on. And, even though this is an element sometimes more noticeable by its absence (as Bill Shankly once said of soccer: it is more important than life and death), this is hardly a feature we want to suggest as critical to our analogy. We hope sociology will be fun but this is hardly something we can insist upon. None the less, there is something in this which is perhaps worth remarking upon.

THE INVENTIVENESS OF GAMES

Earlier we spoke of games as activities done according to rules. However, this quality, important and essential as it is, should not detract from another quality that games display and one which we want to incorporate into our picture of sociology 'games'. Games are, we want to suggest, occasions for inventiveness: a quality not necessarily tied to the invention of new games, though this is certainly involved, but also to the drive to find new ways of playing old games, as in seeking variations in style, play, modifying rules to make them more entertaining, devising new tactics, honing new skills, and so on. Games manifest inventiveness and changeability. Someone is always trying to find new versions of old games, trying to invent new ones: an urge, to put it this way, of finding new ways of going about old activities.

Inventing new ways of seeing things is an important element in the progress of any discipline. As far as natural science is concerned, to pick just a few examples, we have only to consider the way in which Einstein turned around the Newtonian conception of the universe by dispensing with the requirement of the synchronicity of events, or how Marx changed our conception of social structure and process by overturning the view, so beloved of the classical economists, of the inherent rationality of capitalist economic life, or the way in which Darwin changed our whole picture of the origin and relationship between species. We do not want to suggest for one moment that these 'inventions', and they are only one or two of the more glamorous ones, were easily arrived at, or that inspiration alone is all that matters. There are, as we have said earlier, constraints involved in demonstrating how the inventiveness results in ideas which turn out to be significant and important. Not any old invention will do. However, we do want to suggest that the search for novel ways of presenting social life is a useful way of thinking about sociology and its 'games'. That is, we can regard sociology as a discipline concerned with, among other things, the invention of new ways of representing social activities and institutions: it is, if you like, playing with ideas about what social life is like. Marx, Durkheim, Weber, Parsons, Goffman, and others have all tried to turn the sociological project around, sending it off in different directions, and it is this which makes them significant figures in the discipline.

CONCLUSION

What we have tried to do in this chapter is propose what we think is a useful way of thinking about sociology: a way which avoids, or so we hope, many of the vices of the perspectives approach without losing its virtues. We do stress that the game analogy is offered as a way of thinking about *sociology*. In other words, we are not even hinting at the idea that social life itself is a game, though the metaphor has been used in this connection by some sociologists. Our remarks are intended to apply to the discipline of sociology. Thinking about it in this way, using the metaphor as a guide through the massive amount of material and arguments to be found in sociology, may hopefully help to overcome many of the troublesome issues that beginners often find. Not so that the issues are ignored but placed in a form which enables them to be thought about seriously. So, if we find it difficult to follow, say, Functionalist theory, setting it up as a game, as a set of rules and pieces for making moves within such a game, may be a good way of not only seeing how it works, what problems it aims to solve or illuminate, how the moves are made, and so on, but also identify what, by its own standards, it fails to do.

One other warning. In suggesting the game analogy we do not have any particular game in mind. We are not suggesting that sociological 'games' have strong parallels with soccer, or chess, or whatever. They may or may not have, but this is not the point. Games, as we have stressed, vary in so many ways, sufficiently so that it would be highly misleading to select any one game as archetypical of the whole collection of games. Nor is this necessary. All we have done is suggest characteristics of some, perhaps the majority of games, useful for our purposes. There are others, some of which may be equally useful, some less so. But metaphors are not intended to match in every detail the things they picture. They serve to point, to suggest new ways of looking at things, new ways of thinking about matters, and if our analogy does this it serves its purpose. In this connection it is also worth stressing that the game metaphor is not merely another way of talking about perspectives, such that Marxism equals one 'game', Functionalism another, and Interactionism yet another. This is certainly one way in which the metaphor can be used. However, its potential application is wider and subtler than this. We intend it as a frame which can usefully be placed around many aspects of sociological reasoning, including theorising, creating and using data, effecting a comparison between approaches, working through the implications of a theory or a philosophical position, and more. That is, we offer it as a heuristic, a device, useful, or so we hope, for thinking about many of the activities that make up the discipline of sociology. Used in this way it can direct attention to the problems and the point of an activity, its 'rules', the necessary moves or steps, the choices it embodies, the commitments entailed, and so on. In short, it directs attention to the manner in which we can play with ideas sociologically.

FURTHER READING

M BLACK (ed.), *The Social Theories of Talcott Parsons*, Prentice-Hall, 1961. A collection of commentaries and reviews of Parsons' work.

E C CUFF and G PAYNE (eds), *Perspectives in Sociology*, Allen and Unwin, 1979. A good and thorough introduction to the major perspectives currently used in sociology.

N J Demerath and R A Peterson (eds), *System, Change and Conflict: A Reader in Sociological Theory and the Debate about Functionalism*, Free Press, 1968. An extensive collection of papers on the Functionalism versus Conflict Theory controversy.

E DURKHEIM, *The Division of Labour in Society*, Free Press, 1964; *The Rules of Sociological Method*, Free Press, 1967; *The Elementary Forms of Religious Life*, Allen and Unwin, 1968. These are the major works referred to.

M HARALAMBOS, *Sociology: Themes and Perspectives*, UTP, 1980. A comprehensive and popular coverage of sociology organised around perspectives.

R K MERTON, *On Theoretical Sociology*, Free Press, 1967. A classic statement of the Functionalist approach in sociology.

T PARSONS, *The Social System*, Tavistock, 1925. A difficult, long statement of Parsons' theory.

A R RADCLIFFE-BROWN, *Structure and Function in Primitive Society*, Cohen and West, 1952. A classic statement of the Functionalist approach in anthropology.

Chapter 2
SOCIOLOGY AND PHILOSOPHY

In suggesting that we look at sociology as a collection of games we are not, at the same time, implying that it is an activity unsuitable for the attention of grown-ups. Nor are we even hinting that it is some kind of 'con' or dishonest racket. We intend it as a heuristic and one of its most useful features is the way in which we are able to rethink the relationship between sociology and various other intellectual activities. In this chapter we will discuss one such relationship, that between sociology and philosophy. We take this first because it is a source of confusion for many, especially beginners. There is little doubt that some kind of relationship between philosophy and sociology exists, but the uncertainty begins with trying to say precisely what it is, or ought to be. Is, for example, the relationship a master–servant one in which philosophy determines the nature of sociological theories and the aspirations sociology can have to scientific status, or, alternatively, is it an independent one illuminating but not directing these matters. As will become apparent, the use of the game analogy helps avoid being stipulative in these and similar issues and encourages us to examine the variety of alternatives on display. We take it first, then, because it lays the ground for discussions which follow.

One of the main areas where philosophical matters loom large is that concerning whether or not sociology is a science. Most textbooks, and introductory courses, contain treatments of the nature of scientific explanation, the role of theory, the relationship between theory and data, the scientific status of sociology, and so on. Much of this treatment is derived from versions of the philosophy of science and, unfortunately, it is not always clear what the relationship is between these kind of pronouncements and the actual practices involved in sociological work. Until recently many students of sociology, for example, were introduced to Popper's falsification criterion for scientific statements, and the hypothetico-deductive method as the latest philosophical model of what a proper science should look like. Then, as now, it was difficult to see quite how these notions were embedded in the research work to be found in sociological studies. For one thing, it was not clear what one was expected to do with the philosophical model. Use it to criticise empirical studies? Show how seriously they fell short of meeting scientific criteria? Take it as a weapon to beat sociology with, or what? Rarely was it deemed appropriate to use sociology to question the philosophical model. And it is much the same state of affairs now even though Popper is no longer the undisputed arbiter of scientific status. However, this particular issue of the scientific status of sociology we will take up at some length in Chapter 5. For the moment we want to broaden the discussion slightly to look at the role of philosophy in sociology.

Most sociology students' exposure to philosophy is through encapsulations of philosophical views rather than through a systematic and detailed study. The reasons for this are understandable enough. Time is too short to attempt anything like a mastery of sociology let alone relevant disciplines. The danger is, however, that such presentation not only simplifies the assimilation of difficult ideas, but also simplifies the task of criticism by allowing whole bodies of thought to be written of as 'idealist', 'materialist', 'rationalist', 'empiricist', or whatever, without further ado. Condemning ideas, let us note, not so much because they fail to satisfy sociological criteria, though they may well fail by these also, but philosophical ones. Although this 'avoidance of argument' tactic is a misuse of philosophy, it does, none the less, illustrate the way in which philosophy is often awarded a master role in determining what is to count as satisfactory sociology. And, to be fair, it is a role which is not inconsistent with the kind of activity philosophy is seen to be.

The questions which interest philosophers are of a general, and fundamental kind, such as 'What is truth?', 'What exists?', 'What is knowledge?', 'What is morally justified?', and so on. They look totally unlike the questions which concern most scientists; questions which are directed towards finding things out about the world we live in. Further, while science has been strikingly successful, by its own standards at least, in answering the questions it asks, philosophy has been remarkably unsuccessful, or so it seems, at answering its questions. Its debates are renewed in novel guises in each succeeding generation of philosophers in an endless cycle of argument. This, we think, is a strong clue to the nature of philosophical activity.

There is, of course, something of a paradox here. On the one hand, philosophy is often cast in the role of judge and jury deciding upon the intellectual worth of the rest of us, and yet, on the other hand, it is a discipline which consists of endless arguments that go back and forth over the same territory with an awesome persistence. However, in pointing out this paradox we are not suggesting that, somehow, philosophy is deficient.

The point is that it is one of philosophy's essential characteristics that it is obsessively concerned with argument and justification. It would be quite unlike philosophy as we know it if it were to lose this quality. In addition, philosophy's juridical role, while understandable, is something which philosophers themselves disagree about, just as they disagree about the nature of philosophy itself. As we said earlier, if philosophy is given such a role much of the responsibility must be placed on the shoulders of those disciplines who accord it such or, to be more precise, give some philosophical doctrines such a role for, of course, it is not the case that all philosophical doctrines have equal value when it comes to sorting out the opposition.

Here, then, is a first indication of one of the roles which sociology finds for philosophy, namely, that of judge, jury, and executioner in sociological disputes. There are others, as we shall see, but perhaps this is both pre-eminent and characteristic.

SOCIOLOGY AND PHILOSOPHY

There are those who take the view that if sociology and philosophy have anything to do with one another it is altogether too much. Science, including sociology, is distinct from philosophy; indeed, the whole point of creating a science of social life is to get away from speculation and endless argument about society towards an empirical, scientific investigation of it. Others take a different view, arguing that sociology cannot possibly disentangle itself from philosophy. This view can take many forms including the guise, discussed in the previous section, of awarding philosophy a judgemental role in determining sociological worth.

As in so many places in this book we shall not try to judge the rightness or the wrongness of the respective sides to the argument here. We shall simply accept that at the present time both subjects are intimately linked and try to deal with some implications of this linkage. Sociology is currently much involved with philosophy and much that is called sociology is very like, is even the same as, philosophy. This is, from our point of view, neither to be regretted nor proclaimed. It is the way things are.

One of the similarities between philosophy and sociology, although it may turn out to be merely a surface similarity, is that both are thoroughly debatable. There are differences of view at almost every level of sociological work, from its findings to its more metaphysical reflections. And, as we suggested earlier, one basis upon which the student is invited to choose between the different arguments and points of view is often on philosophical grounds: a choice which normally hangs upon the kind of knowledge to which sociology can, or ought, to aspire.

Certainly, one of the perennial questions of philosophy has been, and still is, the nature of knowledge. With the development of science as we know it, this, too, has entered into the argument as a subject of philosophical inquiry, prompting questions concerning the kind of knowledge science provides. At first glance such a question might seem unphilosophical in that it is best answered by science itself, by reeling off the kind of things science tells us. Thus, physics tells us that matter is a form of energy, biology tells us which acids comprise the genetic materials, astronomy that stars are composed of nuclear explosions, and so on. One could give broader characterisations of the sorts of things the different sciences are interested in: physics in the constitution of the basic forces of the universe, biology in the development of life and its forms, and more. However, these answers do not satisfy the question posed earlier for that asks about the nature of the things that science tells us. It is about the significance of the findings of science and how they tell us, if they do, about the nature of the universe around us. In other words, a listing of the things with which the sciences deal does not answer the philosophical question about knowledge or what science tells us about our knowledge of the world.

For example, science, and this is hardly one of its darkest mysteries, tells us what the chemical composition of gold is; but what is at issue, philosophically speaking, is what, when it has told us that gold has a particular chemical composition, has science told us about gold? Is it, for example, telling us that gold has to have such a chemical composition or could we have something else that looks like gold and reacts in all relevant respects like gold, and yet has a different chemical structure? Would this still be gold? Is the chemical structure the essence of the substance, the 'thing' which makes it gold, or is it a matter of linguistic convention? Is it that we call stuff that looks like this and behaves like that 'gold' and if we were to come across some other stuff which looks and behaves like the stuff we have been calling 'gold' but is chemically different, would we call that gold?

Notice here that the scientific facts about gold do not affect the debate. They are not in dispute. The point is, in general terms, that scientific knowledge creates problems that it does not itself answer: problems that are literally 'beyond' science. Although science undoubtedly tells us about the things in the world, it is not always clear what the importance of what science tells us might be. This is one of the tasks philosophers are engaged in and one of the reasons why sociology is also involved in philosophical discussion. In making a proposal for a science of society, what kind of knowledge would we expect to be the result? What kind of knowledge could knowledge of society be? These are the sorts of questions that the prospect of sociological knowledge poses and are still issues which invite philosophical ruminations of one sort or another. And, we hasten to add, this kind of rumination is entirely appropriate and, as we shall point out later, need not involve raising philosophy to the kind of juridical role we discussed earlier in this chapter.

There are, as we have said, many points of view in sociology in answer to the questions we have just posed. To locate and summarise many of the disputes in sociology which are often cast in philosophical terms, we will set up a 'dummy' debate between two opposing tendencies, the 'externalists' and the 'internalists'. The general scope of the argument will be in the broadest terms, but will, at the same time, bring together many issues such as the relationship between theory and method, realism and conventionalism, differences in the kind of constraints which operate in theorising, and the alternative nature of theoretical explanations, all of which are raised and discussed in later chapters.

EXTERNALISTS VERSUS INTERNALISTS

This contrast is designed to crystallise some disagreements which have surfaced in the history of sociology since its beginnings and, before that, in philosophy, and have been directly implicated in many recent controversies about the nature of the 'objects' sociology seeks to know. It is a problem which can be briefly stated as follows: are the 'things' about which sociology seeks to know like the 'things' natural science seeks knowledge about, that is, real, external objects which exist independently of human consciousness, so to speak? This question is not simply to do with the fact that human beings have minds and atoms, molecules, blood vessels, etc. do not. It is a question about the kind of knowledge it is possible, in principle, to obtain about the world, be this the natural world or the world of human beings. Are, then, the 'things' the sciences study 'real' in the sense indicated?

Put this way, most people would fail to see what all the fuss is about: of course the 'things' science studies are real! Nevertheless, there has been, and is, a persistent resistance to this easy answer. The disagreement here can be characterised as an opposition between, as Hilary Putnam puts it, 'externalists' and 'internalists'. The 'externalists' say that the real world consists of some fixed totality of mind-independent objects and that the task of science is to establish a correspondence between our theories and these external things in order to achieve a complete description of reality. The 'internalist', on the other hand, holds that the question about the kind of objects there are in the real world only makes sense within some frame of reference, for example a theory or way of describing, and that there is no way of apprehending the external world without some frame of reference, theory, or description.

As far as sociology is concerned, it is the 'externalists' who have prevailed for much of the time even though, latterly, they have found themselves under attack from a number of quarters. From the point of view of many of its protagonists the 'externalist' argument appears undeniable, except through perversity. There is, surely, a real world out there which can become known to us even though obtaining this knowledge is not a straightforward task. There is, there must be, a difference between how things *really* are and how we, as human beings, *think* they are. It is this difference which gives science its point. By carefully controlled reasoning and assiduous researches we can hone our thoughts and ideas so that they increasingly come to correspond with how things really are. If the world exerts no constraint on our thoughts and ideas or, to put it another way, if there is no difference between how the world is and our thoughts and ideas about it, then science is pointless.

Externalists are not only attached to the idea that it is meaningful to ask what there is independent of our thoughts about it, but also lean strongly towards the idea that there can only be one complete description of what there is. It is a position which also carries along with it more than just an overtone of materialism: that what exists independently of our thoughts, what is real, is fundamentally of a material or physical nature. In the social sciences such assumptions show up in their most extreme forms in doctrines such as 'physicalism' which insists that thoughts, feelings, and all other mental phenomena are really physical events in either the body or the brain. Other and less extreme doctrines of this kind find some difficulty in countenancing the notion of mental phenomena and try to dispose of them by, for example, arguing that they are elaborate ways of referring to physical behaviour. In sum, their position is that everything that can exist must be describable in terms of physics, or some other equally materialist vocabulary, without residue. If anything cannot be stated in these terms, and mental terms seem very different from physical ones, then they must either be ruled out of existence or be translated into acceptable terms, namely physical ones.

Two convictions give the externalist position its very powerful hold: first, the idea that nature imposes our classifications and our theories upon us and, secondly, that there is an indispensable, irreducible, and vital difference between how we think things are and how they really are. If we are to classify reality to say what kinds of things there are, then, from an externalist point of view, what we are about is trying to discover the configuration of things that already exist in the world. If our endeavour is to be successful, one which corresponds with how things are in reality, then it will be reality which will determine this. It is not, in other words, our choice whether a classificatory scheme is successful or not. Something objective settles this, namely, the nature and construction of the things being classified. Nature's own organisation must impose itself upon us and dictate the terms with which classifications and theories must comply. If it is not something objective, if it is not the nature of reality which determines whether our classifications, our theories, do or do not work, then there is nothing to stop the business being wholly arbitrary and chaotic. How is any classification or theory to be judged better than another if it is not in terms of its correspondence with the nature of things?

There are many expressions of this kind of view in sociology, such as the arguments about the objective nature of social phenomea, about the way in which this objective nature is the basis for appraising the different ways of thinking about the social world, about the correspondence of concepts with how things actually are, and so on. And, as we said earlier, it is the externalist idea which seems necessary to give point to scientific inquiry. Moreover, if there is no distinction between how we think things are and how they really are, then this would seem to imply that we can never be wrong; that we can make the world as we choose. Yet, the basis of science is the idea that things are related contingently, that we can, accordingly, be wrong, and to find this out we have to make inquiries into the world. In short, the externalist view appears to be the one required by science, since any other position would call science into doubt and undermine the very things which give it its purpose and point.

Naturally enough, any alternative to the externalist view has to face an uphill task even to demonstrate that it should, at least, be taken seriously. To oppose the externalist seemingly one would have to deny that there is an external world of things and that there is no difference between how things are and how we think they are. Internalists, since they do oppose externalist doctrines, are 'heard' by the externalists as enunciating just such absurdities, and so constituting an irrationalist menace to the point and value of any science including, by implication, sociology. However, as should be reasonably clear from our earlier characterisation of the internalist position, it does not so much deny the externalist claims as argue that its position is misleading because it grossly oversimplifies a complex situation. The internalist argument is that the question of what the world consists in can only be usefully asked within some description or theory, and, far from wanting to doubt science's capacity to discover how things are, wishes to question the externalist's understanding of the basis of science.

The externalist says there are theories and classifications and there are things our theories, and so forth, are about. The theories either correspond with these things or they do not, and the way to decide this is to match the theories against the things. The internalist can admit that this is true enough but that it begs some crucial questions. The internalist does not say that there is no point in testing hypotheses. If a physicist claims that there is a subatomic particle called a 'boson', or a sociologist that the majority of wealth is held by a minority of the population, then the internalist would agree that there is every point in conducting research to see if these things are so. The issue for the internalist arises when we ask how our theories and classifications are to be matched to the things in the external world, for one of the major reasons we are creating theories and classifications is, among other things, to say what kinds of things there are. We want the theories because, presumably, we do not know what kind of things there are; if we did there would be no point to theories and, equally, no point to science. The internalist's primary objection to externalism, therefore, is not on empirical or theoretical grounds but on logical ones. They say, simply, that we cannot know in advance what we are trying to discover and claim that our knowledge is cumulative, progressive, and secured by the facts. The internalist point is not that nothing exists outside of our theories, outside of our ideas, so to speak, but that we can only find out what things do exist from within our theories. We cannot take our theory, our classification, and compare it with the things it is about just like that. We have to decide, *from within the theory*, how it is to be compared with the things it is about. If our theory says that a certain kind of thing exists, say, a 'boson', then we can begin to see if the theory is correct by considering what the theory tells us would have to happen if there was such a particle. How, for example, would experimental observations have to fit with other ideas in our theory to count as confirming the existence of such an object?

The initial objection to externalism, then, is that it makes the matching process sound far too straightforward, that we could compare our ideas with reality by means of observation and decide simply whether or not the two matched. This altogether under-estimates the extent to which theories are wholes, hanging together and, relatedly, the degree to which the nature and significance of observations must be construed within the theory itself. However, the internalists would seem to be in a circle of their own. What they seem to be saying is that the theory tells us what to observe; that is, see only those things which fit the theory. In fact, this is to misconstrue their position. The theory tells us what observations will be relevant to deciding whether things do or do not fit the theory's proposals, not that it dictates its own truth, so to speak. To most of us the records of high-energy physics experiments are meaningless. The pictures of particle tracks appear as a mass of scrawls on the photograph and we recognise that a sophisticated knowledge of physics is necessary to be able to read these pictures as showing the history of particle collisions, their movement, formation, and decay, to know how to tell whether they are signs of the 'boson' we are looking for. The same would hold for the dimension of wealth which the sociologist attemps to measure. In other words, we have to have this knowledge in order to determine the relevance of what it is we are seeing, in order to know what it is we are seeing.

The externalist's response to these arguments is a reservation about the direction in which they lead. They seem to lead towards an unacceptable conclusion, namely, that there are different ways of describing the world. The externalist holds strongly to the view that science is about discovering how reality is. To suggest that reality can be differently described is close to suggesting that reality could be different things too, and this hardly squares with our science let alone our common sense. The internalist, however, does not accept that these conclusions necessarily follow from the argument. The extern-alist talks as if two different theories attempt to describe the same thing, namely, how reality is, and, reasonably enough, if two descriptions are given of the same thing they cannot both be correct. If we say of a block of wood that 'it is two feet long' and that 'it is ten feet long', both of these descriptions cannot be right. However, the internalist's point is that the question of what it is we are describing is not separable from the theory we have and, accordingly, two different theories are often describing quite different things. Talk of the 'same things' is relative to a point of view, what later will be talked of as theoretical and descriptive relevances. Consider the task of describing a woodyard and its contents. We can talk of pieces of wood, perhaps, but of what kind? There is teak, mahogany, oak, plywood, hardboard, pine, etc. and, if the person making the description knows their woods, then it is likely that such a description will be right. But there is another way we could proceed. We could describe the contents of the woodyard as consisting of tongue and groove boards, window frames, doors, wall panelling, and so on. This description, too, can be perfectly sound and correct. As could one which tells us that there are oblongs, rectangles, triangles, semicircles, squares, and the rest.

These descriptions of the content of the woodyard are all, from a point of view, ways of describing the same thing, namely, the contents of the woodyard, but they are not at odds with one another. However, from another point of view they are ways of describing different things: in the example, these would be woods, the things woods are used to make, and shapes, and, no doubt, there could be others. So, the question, 'What kinds of things are there in the woodyard?' is, for the internalist, incomplete without some indication of the point of view from which the description is to be given. The answer depends not only upon what things there are in the woodyard, but on the frame of reference in terms of which we are to effect our description. What makes the difference between one description and another is not solely the things in the woodyard, to put it this way, but the point of view from which they are being considered. Whether it is right or wrong to describe the things in the woodyard according to their substance, or their function, or whatever, is not something that can be decided without reference to a purpose.

If we leave woodyards for the moment and look at what the points just made imply for how we are to regard scientific descriptions, theories, classifications, and the like, then it is more than permissible to suggest that one can respect the classifications and the descriptive language of, say, physics without having to think that this is the only permissible and exhaustive vocabulary. In short one does not have to think that there is, and can be, only one complete description of everything. A classification scheme is, indeed, intended to show what things there are, but it is also, in the normal way of things, intended to *bring out* something about them. For example, in biology life forms can be classified in many ways, including their structural similarities. But, if we want to show evolutionary linkages, then structural similarity may not be the best way of showing this since it could collect together creatures not directly related by inheritance. Bats and wrens both have wings but are not both birds; whales and fish both live in the sea, but the whale is a mammal not a fish. The different classifications do, of course, depend on how things are, but it depends too upon what they are designed to show, to bring out. Nor does this mean that any classification is as good as any other; this can only be decided by reference to some purpose or use. One scheme might well be useless for one purpose, or for any purpose in some cases, or it might be less useful for this purpose than for that. In other words, we can compare and prefer schemes even though we do not have to suppose that one of them is the only possible correct scheme for all purposes.

However, it would be wrong to generalise this point to claim falsely that descriptions are wrong or right only in terms of a purpose; that one is free to describe things just as one pleases. We are saying that our descriptions are constrained by how things are, but that knowing how things are is not simply a matter of effecting a correspondence between theoretical descriptions and the 'facts' because our theories will tell us what counts as such a fit and how we are to recognise it. Referring back to the woodyard for a moment: if we decided to describe the contents in terms of materials, then classifying these as teak, oak, pine, and so on, depends upon knowing how to classify timbers. Being free to choose a frame of reference does not mean that one is free to do whatever one wants within it. Once a frame of reference has been chosen, its application is right or wrong independent of any purpose that inspired it. Nevertheless, the externalist is apt to find unease in such arguments since they seem to introduce an unsettling contingency into science. If science, as a frame of reference, is somehow dependent upon our purposes, and if we had had a different history, and consequently different purposes, then our science might have come to describe the world in a very different way from that at present. It would seem to make science dependent upon the history of our society. Science is the way it is because of our social conventions: little to do with the natue of reality, but with contingent facts about our society. However, by thinking about other kinds of conventional pursuits, we can begin to see just what is intended here.

The Sociology Game

GAMES AND CONVENTIONS

One of the things the idea of the sociology 'game' is meant to do is articulate a view of science as a 'conventional' pursuit. However, we readily accede, for many of the reasons enunciated in connection with the externalist position, this is not easy to accept. Such reasons, in sum, argue that our science is the way it is because of the way the world is: a view that is, by the way, entirely consistent with the notion that science is conventional. Nevertheless, the conventional view of science is a hard one to swallow though perhaps it may be made more palatable if we see exactly what is being claimed by using an example of a more familiarly conventional pursuit, namely, games.

We take it that most will acknowledge that games are conventional activities: they are played the way they are because that is just how we play them. In other words, they could have been otherwise, and, even now, they could be otherwise. It is a matter of our society's history and customs that we play the games we do now; that, for instance, we have football and not baseball, cricket and not boule, and so on. Had someone not picked up and run with a football we might not have had the game of Rugby, and had there not been the differences between the social milieu of the English public schools and the mining regions of the north, we might not have had two kinds of Rugby. Things, in short, could have been different. It is equally incontestable that we do not need to play the games in the way we do. Rugby does not have to have fifteen players a side, indeed one kind has thirteen. It could be played with fourteen a side and with a round ball, and so on. The recognition that all this is so does not discomfort anyone in the way that the suggestion that science is also a conventional pursuit does. The conclusion that some people wrongly draw about the internalists' position is that the results of science are also only conventional; that science is true not because of the nature of reality but because we agree to accept the conclusions as true.

This conclusion is to make a mistake about the relationship between a convention and what is done under it. There are conventions according to which a game is played; conventions which specify what the objectives of the players are, what moves will count as legitimate moves, what events will count as fulfilment of the objectives, and so on. Without agreement on these things we do not have a game. So, although there is a sense in which what happens in, say, a football game is 'dictated' by the conventions, the results of a football match are not the results of agreements, they are not, in a word, conventional. The results are decided by what happens on the field of play, by what the scores are. The same applies to science. Science gives scientists their objectives, tells them what moves will count as legitimate moves, tells them what kind of things will count as the fulfilment of the objectives, and so on. However, none of this means that the results of science are true, if they are, because of convention. They are true because of how things are and stand as the results of inquiries into how things are.

Our discussion so far has made the following points. Philosophy is an acivity in which nothing can be finally settled. Arguments are endemic to it. Moreover, because of the primacy of making and countering arguments in their discipline, philosophers have often been awarded, and have not always been averse to accepting, the role of arbiter of intellectual worthiness. In sociology this has usually been in the form of applying philosophical questions to sociological proposals, findings, and theories. We have suggested that, in the main, such applications have fallen into one of two camps, or, more precisely, tendencies, the externalists and the internalists. In order to take the discussion further we will now illustrate these two broad divisions with reference to a series of debates that have taken place in sociology. These debates can be construed as focusing upon philosophical issues as if these were, or could be, settled with unanimity, whereas, as we have seen in our contrast of externalism and internalism, the philosophical arguments and questions persist. The debates we will sketch are the choice of metaphysical pictures to be utilised, the nature of explanations, and the relationship of philosophy to sociology. As will be seen, the different positions summarised as externalist and internalist predispose very different answers to these questions.

PHILOSOPHICAL ALTERNATIVES IN SOCIOLOGY

We have said a number of times that one of the perplexing tasks the beginning sociologist has to face is making a choice among the variety of ideas about what sociology is like. The discussion of the views of the externalists and internalists has, so far, been concerned with very general ideas about the relationship between our theories and the world: ideas, we suggest, which lurk in the background in the arguments between Functionalism, Marxism, and the rest. One basic way of choosing among the alternatives on offer is to choose the one which corresponds with how things are. The relevance of the externalist views should be fairly clear. There are different accounts of social life, but there can be only one way of describing social reality and, hence, only one of the alternative frameworks, if any, can be right. The problem is to decide which.

Many of the controversies in sociology are conducted as if they must be fought to a finish. Even when students are routinely taught sociology through perspectives, the pluralism this offers is a resigned pluralism, one which takes it as a regrettable fact that sociology is divided into different points of view. Moreover, if one looks at the way in which the alternative points of view carry on their diplomatic relations with each other, it is clear that these are not conducted in a spirit of tolerance but of resentment, churlishness, and, very often, boredom. One reason for this, or so we suspect, is because of the externalist assumptions underlying the comparative assessment of the alternatives on offer. What this means is that sociological approaches are examined as if they project metaphysical pictures of social life.

METAPHYSICAL PICTURES

Ever since Hume wrote his diatribe against metaphysics, the term has acquired an unsavoury reputation. Charging something as 'metaphysical' is often to imply that it is nonsense, worthless, mere speculation, and certainly not to be taken seriously. Here no such meaning is intended. We want to use the term 'metaphysical' to draw attention to a particular attitude towards sociological schemes: an attitude which treats them as if they were intended to fulfil the task that metaphysics characteristically set itself, namely, saying what the ultimate constituents of reality are.

What we have in mind in saying that sometimes sociological approaches are treated as if they were 'metaphysical pictures' can, perhaps, be best illustrated by a dispute which has wide ramifications within the discipline between 'methodological individualism' and 'holism': a manifestation of a much deeper dispute involved in the very idea of sociology, namely, the relation betwen the 'individual' and 'society'. Broadly, what often happens in such disputes is that arguments about methodology develop into arguments about ontology: questions about how we shall proceed become questions about what reality consists in.

METHODOLOGICAL INDIVIDUALISM VERSUS HOLISM

'Methodological individualism', as its title should indicate, is a methodological doctrine; one espoused, for example, by Max Weber and, more recently, by Popper and some of his followers. In brief, it asserts that any statement about social wholes, such as statements about groups, organisations, society itself ought, wherever possible, to be translated into statements about what individuals do. When, to take a simple example, one is inclined to say 'the state nationalised the rail network', one should try to translate this into a statement like 'the functionaries of the state nationalised the railways', though such a statement is likely to be much more complex than this example might suggest. However, the point is that we should not talk in terms of abstract entities but in terms of human beings and their actions.

The reasons for espousing this doctrine are numerous, though a major one is the fear that abstract terms have a habit of taking on a life of their own. If people talk about 'the state', 'classes', 'groups', 'institutions', 'norms', and so on, they will tend to lose sight of the fact that they are also talking about human beings or, more precisely, patterns of association among human beings. Talking about the 'state', say, in a way which makes no mention of those human beings who comprise it, reifies the concept of the 'state'; that is, attributes powers and characteristics to it which properly are those of human beings. This is not only theoretically but politically dangerous in that it might well encourage the view that the state is more important than human beings, and so on.

Against this, 'holism' argues that the methodological individualist programme is misconceived. One cannot translate statements about phenomena such as 'language', 'the state', or whatever, into statements about the actions of individuals without loss of sense and significance. One must, for example in talking about language, refer to the rules and structure of the language which are not restatable as assertions about the speech of individuals. There is, in short, a difference between the organisation of a language and the particular speech of its users. Accordingly, while one does not suppose that a language is something which exists independently of the humans who constitute its community of users, one cannot so simply satisfy the methodological individualist programme however hard one tries.

What we have so far is a methodological argument, one fiercely fought on occasion, about how to get the best understanding of social life and institutions. Unfortunately, it has a tendency to generate arguments about whether there *really* are groups or individuals. This turns methodoligical individualists into asserting that there are *only* individuals; groups as such do not exist but are only fictions. Holism, or some of its varieties, turns out to be maintaining that really there are only structures and that the individual is nothing but the fabrication of structures. The argument is not, then, about methodology any more, though obviously it has methodological consequences, but about ontology and whether individuals or groups are real. As a result, room for compromise or mutual recognition is eliminated. If individuals are, indeed, the only constituents of reality, then the study of 'wholes' is the investigation of phantasms. Reciprocally, if the collective is all and the individual nothing, then there is nothing to which methodological individualism can apply.

The methodological argument does not require the controversy to go in this direction, however. It can recognise that both sides of the argument can have value and that neither need be accepted as a comprehensive doctrine of social science. It can recognise both individuals and 'wholes'. Methodologically, the problem is not which is real, the individual or the group, but what is the best way to understand the nature and relations of individuals and groups? One can argue about this without having to insist that either the group or the individual is real. It may be, depending on the case, that sometimes the holistic strategy is best, sometimes an individualistic one. The trouble with converting this kind of argument into an ontological one is that it makes the two points of view irreconcilable and totally exclusive, as if each were attacking the other's subject-matter. As a methodological controversy it involves disagreement about an approach to a common subject-matter, whatever this might be, not about whether the subject-matter of sociology is the 'individual' or 'society'.

Coexistence, then, is difficult to achieve among different metaphysical pictures. If one says that only social classes are real and that everything is to be explained in terms of their conflicts, then this excludes any approach which does not conceive of social life and its explanation as a product of class conflict. The same would apply to metaphysical Functionalism: if society consists only in institutions with functions etc., then any other alternative is unacceptable. The disputes among sociological alternatives when treated as metaphysical pictures become disputes about what social reality is and what its ultimate constituents are. It is our view that externalist assumptions encourage the reading of approaches as if they were metaphysical pictures: either groups or individuals, to go back to our earlier example, are the ultimate constituents of social life, one cannot have both. The internalist position, however, does not have the same metaphysical attraction. Although it recognises that there can be disagreements among different approaches as to the very nature of social reality, it does not suppose that the differences between them start with such matters, or that it consists only in such disputes.

Approaches involve differences in objectives, priorities, assumptions, strategies, all of which come 'before' disagreements about what there is and which, furthermore, make straightforward comparisons of the different approaches somewhat more difficult than it appears.

From our discussion of the externalist and internalist views of the way in which ideas connect with reality, and also from our discussion of the problems involved in comparing approaches presented in Chapter 1, a major point that emerged is that relationships between two, or more, frameworks have to be considered in terms of whether or not they are looking at the same things, and that decisions on this are relative to a point of view and a purpose. There is a sense in which the alternatives in sociology can be said to share the same purpose, namely, understanding social life or, as an alternative formulation, explaining social phenomena. However, as we have said before, as common objectives these are hardly very specific, saying little about what is actually sought. One could, to return to our game analogy, say that jogging, weightlifting, football, golf are all ways of getting exercise. Unfortunately this does not take us very far since they have little else in common and the exercise they give different. Golf gives exercise to those who otherwise do not get very much, whereas weightlifting is for those who require a lot of muscle-building exercise. So, by analogy, saying that the different sociological approaches can all be said to have the same purpose, more or less, does not mean that they are actually pursuing much the same specific objects.

However, although we might grant that different perspectives, approaches, theories are directed towards different problems, we might still want to claim that on more than a few occasions we are likely to come across *different* explanations of the *same* phenomenon and in this case both cannot be right. We must choose one or the other, or reject them both. What we cannot have is incompatible explanations of the same thing. But, once again, this case is not as straightforward as it looks.

EXPLANATORY RELATIVITY

If we think of explanations as answers to questions then we find in many cases that what look like incompatible explanations are, in fact, answers to different questions. To sensitise us to this possibility, Alan Garfinkel has proposed the idea of 'explanatory relativity' which he illuminates through the following example:

Suppose Alex, after being fired, needs some money to meet expenses until he finds another job. Clyde lends him $300. It seems fairly obvious that there are three different questions (at least) that we would ask with the words, 'Why did Clyde lend him $300?' and accordingly three different explanations one can give for Clyde's lending him $300. The answer might be that this is how much Alex thought he would need; or perhaps Alex wanted more but this is all the ready cash Clyde had available. On the other hand, we may want to know why Clyde *lent* him $300 – Why didn't he just give it to him? Finally, we may be interested in finding out why *Clyde* lent him $300.

The 'same' question might, then, ask very different things, may call for the giving of different kinds of explanation. In the case of Clyde, the explanations that are given do not each explain Clyde's action in such a way that there can be only one correct explanation. Each explains *something* about Clyde's action and they each explain something different about it: why Clyde lent $300 rather than some other sum; why Clyde lent rather than gave the money, and why Clyde rather than someone else lent the $300.

We need to remember, then, that in talking about the 'explanation of a phenomenon' or of a 'theory of a phenomenon', we are, elliptically, speaking of the explanation of *something about* a phenomenon or a theory of *something about* a phenomenon. If we forget this we run the risk of greatly overestimating the extent to which theories and explanations are trying to do the same thing and thus the extent to which they are in *direct* competition with others. Theories and explanations may conflict with each other, but we need to look and think hard before deciding that they do. For example, as we discussed in Chapter 1, Functionalism is frequently condemned because its explanations of institutions preclude historical explanations of them. But the question, 'How do we explain an institution?' does not ask only one thing. Crudely, there are at least two questions here which ask quite different things about institutions. One asks about the existence of institutions, the other about the persistence of them. The first might well require a historical answer, the other may not. If we want to ask *how* an institution comes into being in the first place then a historical answer might well be in order, whereas if we want to ask why an institution comes into being at all, or why, once come into being, it persists, then a Functionalist answer may well suit. There is room, here, in other words, not just for different answers but for quite different kinds of answers.

Of course, if sociological approaches are understood as metaphysical pictures, then they are going to be seen as pursuing the same objectives and their answers as directly comparable. Whether or not they ask or answer the same questions is going to be seen as a measure of their respective suitability. The fact that one approach leaves out of account something that the other includes is likely to make the former seem incomplete by comparison with the latter. What we are arguing for here is a much more 'problem-centred' conception of sociology, one which recognises that there are not just different approaches, but that there are different approaches to different problems. In which case, comparing them is no easy matter. The idea of them as metaphysical pictures makes it seem that the best way to compare approaches is to compare each with reality and see which matches up best. What we have tried to do in our discussion of the externalist and internalist conceptions is to show that such an assumption, such a procedure, fails to recognise the necessary complications, the inevitability with which we must ask questions such as, with what problems in mind, for what purposes are we to compare these schemes with each other and with reality, whose scheme is to be used to specify what reality is like when, after all, it is on just this latter question that the schemes compete?

PHILOSOPHY AS METHODOLOGICAL RECOMMENDATIONS

There is no necessary reason why the solution of philosophical problems should be a precondition for sociological work. Indeed, as the history of philosophy exemplifies, there is a strong sense in which it could be said that philosophy 'feeds off' the practices of other disciplines which have already tried to solve their problems in their ways. The philosophy of science, for example, did not precede science but commented upon existing work and procedures. As we suggested earlier in this chapter, one of the matters with which philosophy deals is the signficance of what various disciplines say, how they choose to say it, and what, thereby, they commit themselves to by way of knowledge, truth, the constituents of the world, and so on. In this sense philosophy stands as an attitude of reflection, an overview to see quite what it is we might be doing in doing, say, physics, painting, enunciating a moral doctrine, or, for that matter, sociology.

It is, of course, through this route that philosophy is often accorded the arbiter role we have already noted. And, naturally enough, is largely responsible for the unsettling effect philosophy so often has. However, understandable as it is, such unease is not the only response. We could, as an alternative, turn philosophical doctrines into methodological recommendations, or agendas, rather than treating them as rather superior reflections on a discipline.

By 'methodological recommendation' we refer to a practice of converting philosophical, or metaphysical, doctrines into proposals for constituting sociological programmes of researchable problems. In terms of the game analogy, it is a matter of choosing to treat philosophical arguments as proposals for designing a sociology 'game' or 'games'. Note that not all philosophical doctrines will be obvious candidates for such treatment. Even if they are, it does not guarantee that the result will be researchable problems or playable games. Note also that we speak of this strategy as a choice, a deliberate decision to treat philosophical views in this way in order to see better where they might lead *sociologically*. Seen in this way, we might perhaps make better sense of, for example, Durkheim and Weber, to mention but two major figures in sociology. What is especially interesting in these cases, and one could easily add Marx to this list, is that they endeavoured to buttress the philosophical underpinnings of social scientific inquiry along with efforts to see how these worked out as programmes of research. To use the game analogy again: they were trying to design sociological 'games' by specifying pieces, the moves that can be made with them, the criteria of winning or losing, and so on.

Thus, Durkheim's philosophical conclusions about the nature of science were turned by him into a set of sociological 'game rules' embodying the idea that if sociology was to be a science in the same mould as the natural sciences then it had to follow the same principles. According to Durkheim, science was the observational study of 'things', aimed at producing accurate descriptions of them, classifying them, and causally explaining the relations among them. These 'things' possessed objective attributes existing independently of the subjective orientations of the observer. The attributes of 'things' were given in 'sensation', the basis, according to Durkheim, of all scientific knowledge. Each science, moreover, including sociology, dealt with its own particular domain of 'things'. Thus, as proposals, Durkheim can be treated as recommending that the study of social reality be governed by the following 'game' rules: first, deal only with the objective attributes of 'things', or 'social facts'; second, describe and record their qualities; third, classify them according to their observable differences and similarities; fourth, investigate the causes of their nature and variety; fifth, by induction, arrive at general laws, or statements of constant concomitance which exist among the 'social facts'. One consequence of these 'rules', and a major difference between this 'game' and the kind of 'game' Weber proposes, is that 'social facts', such as language, culture, fashion, suicidogenic currents, etc., the very stuff of sociological investigation, are taken to exist in their own right beyond, so to speak, individuals. The meanings the members of society entertained about their own social world were often ill-founded, if not distorted. 'Social facts' have to be discovered by the application of a properly scientific method. In other words, the kinds of phenomena that Weber proposes for his 'game', such as meaning, motives, reasons, purposes, and other subjectivities, have little part in Durkheim's 'game'. 'Social facts' are produced out of the associational activities of individuals and exist in their own right independent of individual manifestations of them and, moreover, were connected by causal relations at this level. Of course, such a programme, no matter how carefully worked out, does not apply itself. It has to be worked through, in detail, and with no little effort. In Durkheim's case this resulted in his celebrated study of suicide in which he tried to show that suicide could be treated as a 'social fact' and that the types of suicide varied systematically with other social facts, notably social solidarity.

It does not matter here whether Durkheim was philosophically correct about science, or whether he himself played the game he designed well or badly. Our point is that turning philosophical doctrines into 'methodological recommendations' can be a fruitful and sociologically relevant way of dealing with them. Other movements in the social sciences can be looked at similarly. Behaviourism, for example, is a philosophical doctrine as well as an established research tradition, especially in psychology. As an ontology, behaviourism tells us that the only legitimate entities are those which are publically observable physical and physiological facts about human beings. In this sense, of course, it is a metaphysical picture and one which generates all the endless disputation that we can expect with such pictures. However, we do not need to become embroiled in behaviourism in this way to make it interesting. If we turn it into a game, so to speak, it tells us that its theories must only deal with these publically observable variables and not with mental and subjective entities. These are not allowable pieces in the game. The task now is to see how far this can go in solving the problems, meeting the objectives, it sets for itself. It may or may not go very far, but this is not to be judged in advance. After all one may be surprised.

PHILOSOPHY AND SOCIOLOGY

The discussion in this chapter has focused around the internalist–externalist controversy as a way of illustrating some aspects of the relationship between philosophy and sociology. Of course there are many more connections that could have been drawn, so in this sense the treatment has done less than justice to the general relationship between the two disciplines. However, this is not entirely due to reasons of space, but for the particular reason that general statements about the relationship between bodies of thought, such as disciplines, though often pithy, to the point, and respectable enough in certain circumstances, are *general* statements. As such they ignore, gloss, or otherwise minimise the complicated, changing, and essentially debatable connections there are to be drawn, as we said before in Chapter 1. One could choose any two disciplines and provide a general statement of their relationship. The problem is that when one begins to look in detail at the possible connections, the global characterisations begin to collapse and lose much of their initial informativeness. General statements are, after all, just that, and can be quibbled with from any *particular* position. What would we want to say, for example, about the relationship between sociology and biology? There are many who would argue that these disciplines are as different as chalk and cheese, while others would say that there are strong commonalities, some exemplified in the relatively recent discipline of sociobiology. However, our point is that matters such as these are not all or nothing, and nor should they be treated as if they were. To use the game metaphor for a moment, cricket and football are very different games, yet they do have some things in common: both are played by teams of players, use a round ball, are played on pitches, and so on. The important point is, however, the significance of the commonalities, the significance, too, of the differences, both being, as we continually stress, debatable matters. So as far as philosophy and sociology are concerned, it is not the case that the relation between them is a unitary, all-encompassing one. Philosophy as a whole does not have a relationship with sociology as a whole, except in the most general of terms. Rather, a better way of stating the matter is that some philosophical arguments have a bearing on some sociological arguments.

The discussion has also emphasised that while many of the issues in sociological thought are arguments about philosophical matters, it does not follow, as a general rule, that all depend upon the solution to philosophical questions. In other words, we wish to resist the idea that philosophical questions must be settled before one can get down to sociological work as such. The idea that there are philosophical preliminaries to sociological work which need to be resolved before sociological work proper can begin, is a persistent one. If there is a method which provides assured knowledge, then it would be foolish for sociology to work in any other way: another way of stating the juridical position of philosophy. However, as should be clear from the quickest survey of sociological work, the search for a sound sociological method simply opens up sociological disagreements. It is a search which starts methodological controversies rather than solving methodological problems. Philosophy has been arguing about the externalist–internalist views for a long time without final resolution and there is no reason to expect that the issue can be settled now to enable sociology to decide which is the right one to adopt. Philosophical arguments are only a waste of time if they are undertaken on the assumption that their solution is an essential precondition for the solution of sociological problems, since it forces the choice upon us of either taking philosophy seriously or sociology seriously.

We have been concerned to press the cause of the internalist position in this chapter, but not because we think that it is demonstrably the correct one. We have sought to show that whatever else is claimed for it, it is a reasoned position, that a case for it can be made, just as a case can be made for the externalist point of view. At this stage in sociology's life, the importance of the internalist case is that it encourages a different attitude to the variety of viewpoints which comprise the discipline; one which recognises the autonomy of the various approaches and a more relaxed attitude to their coexistence. It may indeed be nice to have a unified framework but this is of no value in itself. It is only worth while if the framework is capable of satisfying the legitimate demands that can reasonbly be made of it. The trouble in many of the humanities has begun not because of the collapse of such a unified framework but because of the premature efforts to impose one. The variety of sociological approaches indicates a diversity of problems and interests greater than any one of them can cater for alone, and recognition of this will ease the tensions and, perhaps, lead to a better understanding of each of them. There is more discretion involved in the choice of philosophical footholds and sociological approaches, and, accordingly, lots of places from which to begin the development of rigorous and systematic sociological ideas. There is more room for stipulation than is usually recognised or admitted, and preserving this variety is perhaps as important, at the present stage of sociology's development, as a premature choice of what the 'truth' is to be.

FURTHER READING

R BEEHLER and A R DRENGSON (eds), *The Philosophy of Society*, Methuen, 1978. A volume containing some useful papers on philosophical matters in social science, especially those by Winch, Cook, and Taylor.

A GARFINKEL, *Forms of Explanation*, Yale University Press, 1981. For a discussion of the notion of 'explanatory relativity' and a contribution to the individual versus structure debate through an analysis of the logic of explanation.

H PUTNAM, *Reason, Truth and History*, Cambridge University Press, 1981. For a discussion of the 'externalist' and 'internalist' distinction.

A RYAN, *The Philosophy of the Social Sciences*, Macmillan, 1970. Still a good introduction to many of the philosophical issues in social science.

P WINCH, *The Idea of a Social Science*, Routledge, 1958. An exposition of a view that the study of society must be philosophical in character. Also deals with other relationships between philosophy and social science.

Chapter 3

FAIR PLAY FOR THEORIES

In the previous two chapters we have tried to bring out and defend a particular view of sociology by comparing it to a compendium of games. It seems to us that such an analogy encourages an openness of outlook, a willingness to tolerate differences of interest, skill, and taste. We offered a first defence of this view by showing how many of the disputes in sociology could be summarised, in broad terms, as differences over what is to be the body of ground rules of the discipline: should we be externalists or internalists? Our discussion tried to show that neither side has a decisive edge, and if we seemed to advocate internalism as an attractive alternative this was in large measure because it is under-represented in the discipline. In this chapter we shall pursue this theme further. We will defend our analogy further by suggesting that, at present, sociology might be more like philosophy in being an argument subject rather than a knowledge subject and, as such, necessarily pluralistic. One implication of this view is that in comparing theories it is imperative to take each on their own terms and not by, say, comparing them with how things 'really' are, what the 'proper' methods of study are, and the like. We will call this a fair play for theories, and will illustrate by reference to one classic 'dispute' in sociology between Marx and Weber, especially with regard to their characterisation of capitalism. We will show that both offer acceptable but different descriptions which, if taken on their own terms, are distinctive but not necessarily mutually exclusive. Both give, we will say, the descriptions they do because of the theoretical tasks they set themselves.

SOCIOLOGY AS AN ARGUMENT SUBJECT

At present, sociology is more of an 'argument subject' than a 'knowledge' one. The first thing that must be said is that we are not suggesting that 'knowledge subjects' are better than 'argument subjects', or vice versa. We introduce the contrast only for the purpose of drawing out some differences among various disciplines.

By 'knowledge subject' we mean something like physics or, in some respects, like contemporary linguistics, wherein there is a received body of information about the subject-matter of the discipline which is passed on to the incoming student. Thus, in linguistics students will be taught the structure of language, sounds, grammar, and so on. In physics one will be taught the laws of motion, the properties of light, the structure of the atom, and so forth. By contrast, when we speak of an 'argument subject' we have in mind a subject akin to philosophy, a discipline which consists of dissenting points of view. These will normally be presented to the student through the presentation of the different ideas or schools of thought, often in the form of a history of the controversies which have brought the discipline to its present disagreements. The arguments may well be about the very nature of the discipline. Indeed, much of philosophy's argument is about the nature of philosophy itself, and being taught the history of its controversies part of learning what the subject is about. In 'knowledge subjects,' on the other hand, the history of the discipline is inclined to be sharply separated from its present interests.

In saying that sociology is an 'argument subject', we are only suggesting that it is closer to a subject like philosophy than it is to one like physics, at least as matters now stand. This is a long way from saying that it is the same as philosophy, and even further from trying to prejudge the question of whether sociology might change into a 'knowledge subject'. It might develop into a science as hard as any, for big changes do take place, and they can take place quickly and in unexpected ways. For example, it is a little less than thirty years ago that the character of linguistics was changed by the revolutionary work of Noam Chomsky. Sociology might suddenly, and completely unexpectedly, take a similar turn, and though we have good reasons for suspecting this to be unlikely, it cannot be ruled out. Thus, we do not say that sociology cannot aspire to become like physics, nor do we say that it has nothing in common with physics, only that at the present time it is more like philosophy than physics.

Sociology's character as an 'argument subject' is manifested in the diversity of views there are about the nature of the discipline itself. As we pointed out in Chapter 1, the beginning student is likely to find the course organised around different theories, perspectives, or paradigms, the standard ones being Marxism (or Conflict Theories), Functionalism, and Interactionism. Again as we noted before, since these approaches seem to be in fundamental disagreement with one another, one major effect of presenting the discipline in this fashion is to create frustration and bewilderment, or worse, the view that sociology is merely a matter of opinion. There is surely something wrong with a discipline if it cannot agree on a single fundamental approach to its subject-matter.

Of course, if we regard sociology as a 'knowledge subject' such discontents seem fully justified. 'Knowledge subjects' make progress, they go somewhere, learning more and more about the things they study, building up an impressive body of knowledge. Sociology, however, does not progress like this but appears bogged down in disagreements, often fundamental ones, rather like philosophy is 'bogged down' in disputes which, in its case, have been going on for far longer than those in sociology. Sociology has been failing to make progress for merely a couple of centuries rather than the two thousand or more years in which philosophy has been failing. Philosophy goes round its problems time and again, achieving and rejecting resolutions of them, reviewing them, reformulating them, looking at them from different angles, but they remain perennial.

However, because philosophy is not 'going somewhere' in the way that physics is does not mean that it is pointless, or that it fails to achieve anything. Philosophy is doing something. It is thinking about problems which do trouble us and which are difficult to resolve. As we pointed out in Chapter 2, philosophical questions do not admit of definitive answers. Indeed, argument about the answers to philosophical questions is likely to be displaced by argument over the nature of the question itself. Some would say in response to this that if answers cannot be found to such questions, there is not much point in worrying about them. Much better to get on trying to answer questions to which we can find answers. This is, however, a limited view of the point in and the value of thinking about things. It fails to allow for the possibility that our understanding may require not so much answers to answerable questions, but persistence with those which are resistant to resolution. Putting them on one side will not make them go away, and many of the more intractable questions will continue to bother us just because they do not seem to have straightforward answers. Thinking about them for a long time may bring to light the nature and source of the difficulties which prevent ready solutions. It is as important to understand the difficulties in the way of having straightforward answers as it is to give answers to those questions which can unproblematically receive them.

It is in this sense that we see sociology as having more in common with philosophy as an 'argument subject' than with, say, physics as a 'knowledge subject'. Admittedly, many of the questions sociology asks may look more like those of physics, such as, 'Does social class influence educational attainment?', or, 'Is there a relationship between the hierarchical structure of an organisation and its flexibility in adapting to change?' Both look, and there are many, many more of like character, the sorts of questions to which answers can be given. There might be all kinds of problems involved in finding such answers, but there would seem to be a correct answer to be found. However, these are not the only kind of questions on the sociologist's mind. Indeed, it is often the case that lurking behind a question that looks straightforwardly factual is another, rather different, and much more problematic question. In other words, many of the questions which concern sociology are questions which have a philosophical character. For example, one of the issues that concerns sociologists is that, in attempting to create a sociology, they are studying their fellow creatures which makes questions such as, 'How are we to think of our fellow creatures?', 'What attitude are we to take to them?' fairly prominent. Is there a right attitude? As in the philosophical case, the argument can become as much about whether there is an answer as about any content such an answer might have. It is the kind of question one circles around, examining it in different lights, on the basis of different assumptions, related to different issues, and so on. Though this process does not progress towards one generally accepted answer, towards a point at which the question can be decisively closed, none the less, one comes to appreciate more the issues involved, the range of positions that can be taken, the difficulties in the way of neat solutions, and so on: in other words, seeing matters a little more clearly than hitherto.

As we have remarked, there are many who think sociology is in a state of crisis as evidenced by the diversity of ideas and the extent of disagreement. It is rare to find anyone, as we do, who finds the diversity both desirable and encouraging. More common is the feeling that there is something, some *one* thing, wrong with the discipline and if this could be identified and put right, then sociology could begin to make progress. For reasons we have already discussed, we do not find the fact of disagreement in the least disturbing, but take it as something which is only to be expected. Rather than indicating a deep and fundamental crisis, it simply demonstrates the need for more, and innovative, thought about the matters over which there is disagreement. Agreement is not, in and of itself, a virtue. The idea that one should avoid and eliminate disagreement just for the sake of achieving unanimity is quite out of order in intellectual matters, It is, as Aneurin Bevan once said in a different context, the unanimity of the graveyard. If sociologists are to reach agreement, the best way to do this is not necessarily by looking for something that can be agreed upon, but by cultivating disagreements, seeing them right through, taking them seriously and working them out expeditiously.

It is in this connection that the recognition of sociology's character as an 'argument subject' is most helpful. Thinking of it as a 'knowledge subject' simply makes it seem inadequate in comparison with the more well known of 'knowledge subjects' which go on heaping up findings year after year. Seeing sociology as an 'argument subject' allows us to suggest that although it may not be accumulating knowledge in the same sense as, say, physics, it is learning something. Accumulating knowledge, to put it this way, in the manner of, for example, physics, is only one way of learning. There is at least one other way which may be called 'dialectical', and is the kind exhibited in the Socratic arguments. It is a learning which comes through the confrontation and interchange of different points of view; a process not necessarily leading to any kind of agreement, but certainly involving the development and articulation of the various ideas, leaving one, at the end, somewhat wiser than before. One can learn from a subject like sociology where there is no fundamental agreement, no one unifying framework of thought but only disputing schools. And we shall learn more if we assume at the outset that there are reasons for such disagreements; that they are not, in other words, the result of mere error, wilful stupidity, ideological blindness, or a lack of thought.

What is wrong with sociology, then, is not that it has been wracked by disagreement but, rather, that the disagreement has so often been unproductive. One source of this is, we believe, the attachment to the idea that sociology is a 'knowledge subject' which means that the disagreement has been driven by the notion that one framework of thought must dominate the discipline if it is to have coherence. In other words, the objective of the argument has generally been, to repeat, the elimination of rivals. However, the range of interests which can legitimately be taken in the subject, the demands made of it, the host of problems which it has raised, are all too numerous to be dealt with by any one of the extant sociological approaches. No one of these can fulfil the requirements that may reasonably be made of sociology, and different approaches will inevitably develop as new demands are made of it. The subject is, in a word, pluralistic: at least for the present.

CHOOSING AMONG THE ALTERNATIVES

At this point we want to continue with a theme we have addressed in both the preceding chapters, namely, how to go about the business of comparing, and perhaps choosing, among the alternative sociological approaches? Whereas on the previous occasions the discussion largely provoked a consideration of other matters, in what follows we shall attempt to wind the thread more tightly and deal with such a comparison.

It might seem a prime obligation of a book such as this to make the business of choosing among the alternative approaches easier rather than difficult by making it plain what is essentially at stake between the different positions, which ones are most in accord with the facts, and so on, so reducing the elements of comparison to as few as possible. However, we think that there has been altogether too much of this simplification and easing of decisions. So much so that the difference between simplifications useful for elementary teaching purposes and adequate characterisation of issues and views has been obscured. There is, of course, much to be said for simplifying the complex entanglements of sociological arguments in order to give the student an entrée into the discipline. It is, however, often forgotten that these simplifcations are made for teaching purposes and, instead, come to be treated as though they were complete and exhaustive characterisations of the points of view available and, moreover, adequate grounds for the making of reasoned and mature choices.

It is not our aim, then, to pretend that there is little for the student to think about before deciding which approach, if any, is the correct one. Rather, our aim is to provide a reminder of the difficulties involved in making thoughtful choices and to encourage much more hesitancy in choosing, much more consideration of the alternatives before deciding which has the decisive advantage. Above all, we would like to discourage the practice of comparing all alternatives from the point of view of one, of failing to take the different ways of approaching sociology independently of each other, of neglecting to understand each on its own terms and avoiding invidious comparison: in short, discouraging the unfair treatment of theories and approaches. It may, of course, be the case that different approaches exist because some people are too dim to see the obvious: cannot see the simple truth that, for example, Marxism, or Interactionism, is right and the only possible way of thinking about human society. Equally well, it might not be the case. After all, 'a way of seeing is also a way of not seeing', to borrow Kenneth Burke's fine phrase. In which case, the Marxist point of view, and indeed any other example, while it opens one's eyes to certain important aspects of social life, cannot take in them all and, indeed, demands that many things be disregarded.

THE IMPORTANCE OF CHARITY IN INTERPRETATION

It is easy to make a choice if it can be made on the assumption that one side has all the right answers. It is more difficult if no one side has all the advantages; if it can be seen that all the alternatives have their legitimate tasks and preoccupations. In which case, any choice will involve 'opportunity costs'; that is, having to sacrifice some desirables in order to obtain others. Making a choice is also easier if the alternatives are presented as rivals, as if all were competing for the same space and only room for one. This view we have already dealt with in some detail.

We are not convinced that making the choice easier is the right way to proceed. We are not convinced especially that projecting the various approaches as rival general pictures of the social world, as though each were a general theory for sociology, is the best way forward. As we have emphasised elsewhere, what you see is not just dependent upon what there is, but also upon the point of view you take and it is, therefore, inevitable that the approaches seem very different things: the frames of reference through which they see are different.

One of the difficulties in relating different frames of reference is that there are basic problems of mutual understanding involved; problems not unlike those involved in translating between different languages and cultures. In this connection it is argued that meaning and belief cannot be separated. What we understand someone to mean by an expression depends upon what we understand him, or her, to believe. If someone says, 'I'm a dead duck', then we might understand him to be speaking idiomatically if we think that he cannot literally believe himself to be a duck's corpse. He must mean that he is beaten, has been found out, or something similar. If, on the other hand, we have reason to suspect the person is mentally ill, then perhaps we might infer that he does mean it literally, that he does believe he is the embodiment of a dead duck. The example is not serious but the problem it illustrates is. If what is meant depends upon what is believed, and if what is believed is discovered through an understanding of what is meant, then our capacity to translate will depend upon the assumptions made about beliefs. If we make certain assumptions about someone's beliefs, we will translate their meaning one way. If we change these assumptions then the translation will be different. It goes the other way, too. If a certain meaning is assumed then we will be disposed to read what they say as implying certain beliefs; beliefs which are different than if we took their meanings otherwise. So, to translate we have to make assumptions about meanings or beliefs, or both and, depending on the assumptions, the results of the translation will vary.

So, in interpreting something whose intelligibility is unclear, to break the circle of assumptions needed about meanings and beliefs, i has been suggested that we operate with a principle of charity. That is we can adopt a policy of interpretation which will seek to make the best sense of unintelligible expressions in terms of our own under standing of what is sensible and rational. If, for example, we find an expression which seems nonsensical, then we can assume some beliefs which are like our own and which would, thereby, enable us to make some sense of what is being said. It might lead us, for instance, to treat the puzzling expression as metaphorical rather than literal or as performing some other role within the language. If we are not charit able then we shall make no effort to find a rationality to what is being said, will make no allowance for the possibility that we are assuming the wrong meaning or background of beliefs: all we are simply doing is, in effect, asserting that it makes no sense and that is that. O course, we need to add here that although sense can be made out o most things, it does not follow that it is correct. We are not claiming that the effort to give a charitable interpretation of theories and approaches will somehow make them true. Charitableness in interpre tation is not some wonderful instrument that will solve all our problems. Nevertheless, before we can properly decide upon the truth of a theory, the fruitfulness of an approach, we must first make sense of it. And, whether a framework makes sense or not has much to do with the effort we are willing to invest in trying to interpret it.

This kind of charity can be seen in the interpretation of Hegel, a philosopher who is known to sociology mainly through the work of Marx. For a long time Hegel was interpreted by many, Marxists and anti-Marxists alike, as a buffoon putting forward wildly improbable theories about how ideas decided the course of history. Marx had taken over the form of Hegel's argument but had to turn its content upside down, pointing out that it was human labour which shaped history and not ideas. Uncharitable treatment was meted out to Hegel by interpreting him in ways which emphasised his insistence on the importance of ideas and making him appear absurd and ridiculous. Interpretations, however, tend to go in cycles, and the persistent denigration of someone like Hegel is likely to lead, at sometime, to a review of his work in order to see if he is as bad as alleged. The result of this more charitable treatment is that recent interpretations of Hegel stress how close Hegel was to Marx, pointing out that his work does recognise and emphasise the role of human labour in the shaping of history. Nor does his emphasis on ideas comprise quite the absurdity it has so often been made out, for it transpires that it is not at all a theory about the independent, autonomous evolution of ethereal things called 'the Idea', 'the Spirit', or 'the Mind'. These are only, so to speak, collective nouns for the products of the lives of real, concrete human beings of the kind Marx wanted to talk about. They are no more ethereal or non-existent than the 'classes' which are Marx's collectivities.

Reading Hegel charitably, that is, in light of what we now take to make sense, results in a much more 'materialist' interpretation and one which is much closer to the Marxian scheme than previously supposed. One of the great beneficiaries, of course, of charitable reinterpretation is Marx himself. In the 1950s and early 1960s Marx was treated in sociology as little more than a historical curiosity. His analysis of capitalism, for example, plausible for its time but falsified by social changes that he had failed to predict. Against this kind of glib dismissal, a rereading of Marx showed that he was not a simpleton, that his theories were neither crude nor as obviously erroneous as they were made out to be. Indeed, his theories can be reread, quite often, as anticipating later developments on and improvements in his own thought. Consequently, sociology found that its dismissal of Marx had been, at least, premature and that it was necessary to go back and come to more adequate terms with it. So, to the extent that sociological thought does display a lack of charity, the least consequence of this is that there will continue to be 'regressive' movements in sociological thought as people find that premature termination of a particular approach or set of problems grievously underestimates the tasks it presented. The lack of charity forces the need for reinterpretation and the impression of progress is only an illusion.

We will now try to explore some of the problems involved in assessing alternative approaches to sociology ensuring fair play for each of them by comparing Marx with Weber, a standard example. We choose this because it is not only a common one in the discipline, but also because it is one which often leaves much to be desired. In this instance we feel that it is Weber who has been less than charitably treated, though this is not to lay the fault entirely at Marxism's door. A mere twenty years ago it would have been necessary to be more sympathetic to Marx since his opponents overestimated their capacity to defeat his arguments. The situation has now changed and it is Weber, Durkheim, Parsons, among others, who are in need of more sympathetic treatment.

A COMPARISON OF MARX AND WEBER

The first point to make is that any theorist can be interpreted in different ways, and if the recent and more sympathetic treatments of Marx have done much to improve our understanding of his work, it has done nothing to make him any more conclusively interpreted. There is no shortage of interpretations which agree that Marx is an important, if not the most important, contributor to social thought, but there is less agreement on what it is that makes him so. We cannot enter into, and barely have room to allude to, the difficulties in Marxian scholarship. All we can point out is that there is a range of interpretations stretching from the relatively uncontroversial to those which are thoroughly debatable. For the purpose of our discussion the themes which are especially relevant are those to do with the question of economic determinism, idealism, and historical necessity.

Economic determinism

There is little doubt that Marx gives economic relations an important position in the understanding of society and its workings. Irrespective of how this is eventually worked out, there is no question that for Marx understanding the structure of economic relations is fundamental to understanding the nature of a society, and it is on this point that the fullest range of interpretations have centred. The range stretches from the readily acceptable claim that economic relations limit the possibilities of social life to the stronger claim that there is a specific causal connection between economic structures and other elements of social organisation.

The first of these claims argues that the capacity of a society to maintain, for example, a standing army depends on the ability of its economy to produce a surplus over and above the requirements of those directly engaged in production, in order to provide those engaged in military service with a livelihood they will be unable to produce themselves. If everyone has to be engaged in production to meet their own survival needs, then they cannot engage in full-time military service. This is a relatively uncontroversial claim and one applicable to many areas of social life other than the example of standing armies. The capacity of people to arrange their affairs in particular ways presupposes that they have the economic wherewithal to do this. Nowadays, this is a claim few would dispute. The social life we lead is one which is, in many broad and diffuse ways, affected by the kind of economy we have. At the time Marx offered his work, it would not have been so indisputable. The idea that we might want to study art, religion, literature, and so on, by relating them to the economic structure of society would be much harder to take than it is now, when it is common for scholars, Marxists and non-Marxists alike, to look to the socio-economic context of artistic and other activities for understanding.

We can, accordingly, read Marx as making what is now an inoffensive 'heuristic' suggestion about a strategy social inquiry might adopt for understanding a wide range of social phenomena, including many which might seem far removed from the economic spheres of life. However, Marx can also be read as offering a much more controversial proposal, one which could be described as 'economic determinism', namely, that there is a causally determinate relationship between the economic and other structures in society. Thus, in Marx's distinction between 'base' and 'superstructure' which treats economic relations as basic and others, such as legal, familial, religious, and political ones, as a superstructure erected on that base, there is a strong suggestion of a one-way connection between them: the form of other social relations being determined by economic ones. This is, of course, a much bolder claim than the previous one we discussed, and is vastly more contentious. It can be admitted that social relationships do require certain kinds of economic preconditions for their possibility without also requiring that there be some strict causal connection between economic and other social relations.

The suggestion that the economic structures and its forces determine the form of other institutions in specific ways is an interesting idea; much more interesting than the bland, uncontentious claim that the parts of society affect each other, or that the economy serves as a precondition for other social activities and institutions. However, it is also much less plausible: a not uncommon situation in sociology where often the interest of a claim is inversely related to its plausibility. Be this as it may, there are remarks in Marx's work, and in that of his collaborator, Engels, which suggest that he is advancing this bold and original thesis. However, remarks can also be found which suggest that this strong claim is not seriously intended. Engels, for one, is famous for his qualifying comments that 'only in the last analysis' are economic conditions to be regarded as fundamental, and for recognising that it is the interaction of all the parts of a society which determine its actual character.

This is all well and good. What is not acceptable is to treat work which justifies the claim that there is a diffuse interconnection of economy and society as though it justified the stronger claim that there is a specific causal connection between them. One cannot oscillate between these two claims, putting forward the bold one where it is to advantage, but substituting the more acceptable one where the former runs into empirical trouble. Engels especially, seems to want his cake and eat it too by suggesting that economic relations are only one set among others in society, yet, at the same time, insist that they are, somehow, more basic than other relations.

So, as far as our comparison of Marx and Weber is concerned, if we take Marx as advancing the less bold thesis, the more plausible one, that economic relations are important in social life, then there is little difference between them. Weber is no less convinced than Marx that economic relations are important to our understanding of society and its workings. He also emphasises that there cannot be a simple and one-sided connection between economic and other social phenomena, but numerous and multifarious connections between them. As far as the connection between economy and society is concerned, Weber presents us with a varied and highly complex classification of such connections. Economic organisations, economic positions, economic interests all have an important impact on other aspects of social life, and it was part of Weber's interest, just as it was of Marx, to understand how. But if we use the Marx of the bolder thesis, namely, as advancing the position of 'economic determinism', then there is a wide gulf between him and Weber. Weber does deny that economic relations are the only determinate and influential forces in history, though this denial is not one intended to minimise their contribution, but only to deny that they have exclusive sway. But, as we have seen, there is no need to understand Marx this way either. His account can be seen as one which was, perhaps, exclusively focused on economic relations and their effects without supposing that he thought that *only* economic relations had any effect upon other social relations. In other words, Marx could be interpreted as concentrating on those aspects of social life in which economic relations are influential, so imposing, what we will later call, self-constraints on his theorising; that is, being interested in phenomena only in so far as they can be seen as influenced by economic relations. Restricting theorising in this way to certain kinds of influences does not have to deny other kinds of influences.

Idealism

Both Marx and Weber, then, are agreed that economic relations are crucial to understanding the organisation of society, including aspects which might seem far removed from economic life, such as art and religion. None the less, Weber is often counterposed to Marx as an 'idealist' and, often, for this reason dismissed from serious consideration. The use of particular terms as signals of right and wrong, as in this case, is usually a good index of how far an argument has degenerated. 'Materialist' is nowadays used as a term of approval and 'idealist' a token of abuse, or at least a position requiring apologetic explanation: a measure, again, of how far sloganising has been substituted for thought.

Marx was certainly opposed to Hegelian Idealism which, he felt, postulated history as the development of thought which meant, in practice, the development of art, religious thinking, and, especially, philosophy. Thought developed, or so Hegel could be uncharitably understood to be saying, as if it were something which existed independently of human beings in some ethereal world of its own. Marx, however, was sceptical of Hegel's Idealism or, more accurately, the idealism ascribed to Hegel, for two reasons: first, history is the history of real, actual human beings, not abstractions: second, although Hegel thought that developments in art, philosophy, and so on had brought people to freedom, as far as Marx could see it left them as impoverished and as enslaved as before. Marx could not accept that a philosophical theory, on its own, could so change the world as to set people genuinely free.

For us the question is whether Weber is an idealist in anything like the sense that Hegel is alleged to be. In brief the answer is no. Weber, like Marx, insisted that history is nothing but the history of actual, concrete human beings: there are no 'occult' forces or phenomena over and above those created through the organisation of human beings in association with one another. History is the history of the material life of material creatures. However, Weber does not dismiss the importance of ideas in shaping the course of history. His study, *The Protestant Ethic and the Spirit of Capitalism,* argues not against Marx but against a certain kind of materialism which denied that ideas have any independent role whatsoever, that all ideas, all ideologies, were class determined and only class determined.

One way of understanding the relationship between ideas and, say, the economic structure is embodied in the distinction noted earlier between 'base' and 'superstructure'. In this case, economic conditions are held to represent real material conditions of life, and religion, law, politics, art, and so on, because they are involved with ideas, thought. So, the claim that Marx turned Hegel upside down and reformulated the connection between ideas and material conditions the correct way, temptingly leads to the further view that the relationship between 'base' and 'superstructure' must be of one-way determination. Allegedly, Hegel believed that thought, or consciousness, determined reality, or being, and it was Marx who turned this the right way round by claiming that being determined consciousness. Hence, economic conditions determine legal, religious, artistic, etc. relations and ideas. The only other alternative is idealism. Accordingly, because Weber wanted to give religion an independent role in the explanation of the origins of capitalism, he is seen as an idealist.

However, there is no reason to regard Marx's distinction between 'base' and 'superstructure' as one connecting material conditions to ideas. It can just as readily be seen as a connection between institutional sectors, between the economy and the legal system, religious organisations, the family, and so on: that is, as a general frame of sociological reference. These institutions, collectively, make up the real, material conditions of life for human beings, and to suggest that religion may develop in ways not specifically connected with the economy, is very far from proposing that thought determines being, or anything like it. In so far as the the development of religion is concerned, Weber attempts to give a thoroughly materialistic account of how it is interwoven with political and economic interests, the structures of power and inequality in society, the development of states, and so on, as well as depending on the interests and problems that arise from within religion itself. The history of the institution of religion is the history of human beings' reproduction of it; nothing more, nothing less.

As far as religious doctrines, or any other set of ideas for that matter, making a significant impact on history, Weber is as sceptical as Marx. Weber does put forward a thesis about the Protestant ethic to the effect that it had the unintended effect of creating the kind of motivation that stimulated the kind of activity required to exploit the opportunities provided by the economic and technological conditions favouring the development of modern Western capitalism. However, this was no thesis alleging the power of ideas to transform the world. Weber was most insistent that ideas could only have a real effect if they were associated with the interests of particular social groups. It was the connection of Protestant beliefs to the bourgeois social stratum in particular European countries, that gave such ideas the decisive influence Weber thought they had.

So, if we are going to talk in terms of thought and being, to put it this way, Weber insists that thought is determined by being and not, as he is often portrayed, suggesting, in idealist fashion, that being is determined by thought. He insists that religious teachings, political doctrines, juridical policies, and all other forms of thought are the products of actual, historical, material circumstances. But he also insists that they are the product of complex circumstances in which the economic will figure as one element among many other consequential factors. Thought can indeed be linked to economic circumstances, but not in such a way that the former is a direct outcome of the latter.

This point can be reinforced by reference to the extent to which Weber considered the development of the Protestant ethic as a process independent of the local social and economic circumstances of Reformation Europe. However, this argument is not, as is often thought, about the development of thought independently of socio-economic factors, but about the independence of a set of socio-economic causes from another set. He suggests that the Protestant Reformation, and the course it took, is not to be understood simply by reference to the coexisting social and economic circumstances which affected it. The Reformation, its occurrence and course, needs to be understood in relation to the long history of the Judaic and Greek traditions of the West. The social and economic circumstances which brought religion to the point of the Reformation, and which shaped it so that it would respond as it did, are circumstances which developed independently of those obtaining at the time of the Reformation itself. Hence, the capacity of Protestant sects to provide the kind of stimulus to rational capitalistic enterprise which they did, according to Weber, cannot properly be understood as a response to the local and contemporaneous requirements of a nascent capitalism. The religious tradition had been shaped by the social and economic characteristics of the previous societies in which it dwelt. Weber's argument, then, is that it is the socio-economic conditions of the societies which preceded the Reformation which shaped in important respects the religion which motivated economic activity of the type associated with capitalistic enterprise.

Historical necessity

Another common reaction to the debate between Marx and Weber is to see the latter as propounding an 'accidental' view of history. That is, that Weber is claiming that we cannot scientifically explain why, for example, capitalism arose. In the discussion so far we have been suggesting that there are few major differences between Marx and Weber, especially if we adopt a more relaxed interpretation of Marx. However, the question of the 'necessity' of capitalism is one which could produce significant differences of view between the two.

Weber certainly held the view that capitalism did not have to arise and, further, once arisen could have developed in different ways. His reasoning, in brief, is as follows. The social, political, economic, and technological developments in Western Europe in the pre-Reformation period were certainly of a kind which could have produced the thoroughgoing, systematic, and far-reaching transformation of society which, as a matter of fact, occurred. Those circumstances offered that possibility. But such opportunities are not always taken. Their exploitation requires a motivation to take advantage of them. The mere fact of opportunity does not automatically give rise to such motivation. Consequently, there are two matters about the rise of capitalism which need explanation: the opportunity and the motivation to make use of it. The Marxist account had done much to illuminate the first of these, but had little to say about how the motivation might arise. It could not arise simply because it was required for capitalist activity. It must arise before the development of that activity and, hence, must be understood in relation to circumstances other than those favouring capitalist production as such. It is for this reason that Weber looked to what he regarded as a powerful influence on human motivation, namely, religion.

Without the development of the Protestant ethic, or something very like it, Weber claims that exploitation of the opportunities provided by Reformation Europe would not have taken the specific direction that it did. A capitalism might have developed, but it would have been something very different from the capitalism that did arise. Indeed, without the Protestant ethic, or similar, capitalism might not have developed at all. One important purpose to Weber's comparative studies of world religions and their respective civilisations was to examine why capitalism arose in Western Europe, when it did, and took the form that it did, for it was not the only place where conditions were, or had been, favourable to rational capitalistic activity. It was the only place in which the opportunity so presented had been seized in such a way as to produce a capitalistic economic system with such far-reaching consequences. Traditional China, for one, had many conditions favourable to the development of capitalistic economic activity, though it had failed to grow into the dominant economic form within the civilisation.

So, according to Weber, capitalism did not have to arise. What he did show was that its development was contingent, that is, something that might or might not have happened, and, as such, a respectable piece of scientific work. Science does not have to show that something is determined, that it *had* to happen. The business of science is with things which are contingent. Even scientific determinism does not show that something had to happen, only that given that it did happen there had to be certain predisposing conditions or causes. Scientific determinism, in other words, is conditional not absolute. Absolute determinism is to say that something had to happen, that it is inconceivable that it could not have happened, and that, no matter what, it would have to come about. Marx is sometimes interpreted as an absolute determinist arguing that capitalism had to come about regardless. Whether he is guilty of this or not, this kind of insistence is not a bona fide scientific one.

Nevertheless, one of the standard readings of Marx is to see him as propounding a set of laws explaining the whole of history. The idea that history has some necessary pattern is a Hegelian idea. Hegel set out to show that there was a necessity to history where others had thought there was only contingency. Since Marx was influnced by Hegel there is some basis for thinking that Marx, too, wanted to show the necessary pattern to historical development by showing the successive and fixed stages societies passed through. Nor would he have been alone among the great thinkers of his century in wanting to emulate the principal sciences of his day by discovering the laws that governed society's evolutionary stages. However, as a view of the aims of science and, in particular, the nature of its laws, it is mistaken. The laws of science are intendedly general but work within specified conditions. Given the conditions, if the law is correct, then it will specify the pattern of occurrences which will follow within the domain concerned. That is, a law, a generalisation, will only explain within the conditions set out for it. The theory of evolution, for example, offers principles which explain changes in forms of life; principles which have to do with the natural selection of characteristics encouraging survival of species and their adaptation to environments. But, the generalisations involved, the laws so to speak, do not specify what particular stages a life form must pass through, or even entail that there has to be life or evolution at all. Given there is life, variations in environments, and so on, then life forms are subject to the laws of natural selection.

So, denying that capitalism had necessarily to exist does not mean that Marx and Weber are denied the possibility of formulating something like 'laws' of social development, or that they must accept that the rise of capitalism was 'just an accident'. After all, accidents are entirely explicable as any coroner's jury will attest. Weber's insistence that capitalism's occurrence was entirely contingent is a position entirely compatible with the normal form of scientific determinism. The conditions which favoured the rise of capitalism in Western Europe did not have to exist. Given that the conditions did exist, including the motivating Protestant ethic, then capitalism had to develop. Weber, however, would not have put it quite as strongly as this since he did not think that historical conditions were as determining as physical ones. Nevertheless, the form of his argument is suitably scientific.

The differences, then, between Marx and Weber are not located by us in places where they are usually sought. The critical difference is not that one is a materialist, or economic determinist, and the other an idealist, for, in most respects, neither is more nor less materialist than the other. The difference lies elsewhere, most plausibly in the assumption that there is some overall pattern to history and the development of society: the view that there is some necessity to the course of events, that they must follow the pattern they do in order to fulfil some design built into them. However, even here it is not clear whether Marx was so convinced that there was such a pattern to history, though there are respects, certainly, in which he can be understood as claiming this. Weber, on the other hand, clearly dissociates himself from any such suggestion. It might be more appealing to believe that history is destined to take a certain course and, while we do not say that such a claim is invalid, it is mistaken to think it a more scientific one.

The aim of this chapter has been to illustrate that comparisons can be distorted, in this case of Marx and Weber, by unjustifiably slanting it in favour of one or other of them. By portraying Marx as a thinker realistically aware of the fact that human beings make their own history, of the way in which their institutional lives are rooted in economic conditions, of the ways in which ideals can cloak base interests, developing a schematic account of history but aware of its limitations, expounding general laws but flexible and adaptable in applying them, he can be made to sound much superior to Weber. Weber, after all supposes that ideas are key forces in history, fails to recognise the importance of real material conditions and interests, overestimates the importance of individuals, and thinks that history resists explanation and understanding. Marx certainly is superior to this fictional Weber, but is not much superior to the actual Weber who endorses much of Marx's thinking on the importance and character of economic factors, is well aware of the extent to which economic interests are prominent in history and of the degree to which ideals can disguise and promote material interests, and is just as aware of the extent to which the historical situation of individuals and groups is beyond their control. What else is the study, *The Protestant Ethic and the Spirit of Capitalism*, but an ironic reflection on the way a particular group gave stimulus to the very things they warned against?

When it comes to comparing Marx and Weber there is not a lot to choose as far as their accounts of economic and social change are concerned, and it is this which makes choosing difficult. Though they can paint similar pictures of the course of history, they can also draw very different conclusions from them, each with as much justification as the other. Weber agrees with Marx about the origins and the destination of capitalism. Both thought it likely that socialism would be next on the agenda for capitalist societies. However, where Marx anticipated that the coming of socialism would end the evils of capitalism and create a qualitatively different state of human freedom, Weber thought that socialism would amplify the worst tendencies of industrial society and usher in a nightmare world of oppressive and alienating bureaucracy. There are no good reasons *independent of their theories* for thinking either Marx or Weber correct. If Marx's theory is accepted, then the idea that property and oppression are indissolubly linked encourages the view that the abolition of property must also mean the end of oppression. If Weber's view is accepted, that is, that power and domination can take the form of the possession of property but need not do so, then the abolition of property does not imply the end of domination, only of one of its forms. In light of historical experience there is much to be said for both of these positions, and though one might, for reasons such as optimism, philosophical preference, and so on, like one of these more than the other, taking it up in this way does not invalidate the alternative.

CONCLUSION

Pitrim Sorokin is a sociologist whose work is little noticed these days even though he has written a number of amusing books, including a very critical one, *Fads and Foibles in Modern Sociology*. In this book he makes fun of, among other things, the 'Christopher Columbus Complex' which amounts to arriving at Kennedy airport and believing that one has discovered America. The sociological version of this is, of course, the unwitting discovery of an idea predecessors had already put forward and believing it to be a major breakthrough in sociological thought. Victims of such a complex tend to overestimate our contemporary achievements because they underestimate those of our predecessors, the tasks they faced and, perhaps, failed at, largely because the victims of the complex have not tackled those tasks themselves. This kind of mistake is prevalent in a discursive discipline such as sociology. It is difficult to read exhaustively, even in one field, especially if one is interested in getting on with sociological work as opposed to becoming a scholar of its history and writings. Inevitably, one will remain ignorant of much of sociology or only aware of it through secondary sources, selective reading, and casual interpretations. In which case it is even more important that there is room for charity in interpretation.

We are not recommending that in all cases the maximum amount of charity is exercised in the interpretation of sociological ideas since, on occasion, there is need for uncharitable interpretation too. Sometimes it is desirable to give a position credit for the best and most sensible argument but, at others, it is fair to withhold this. However, what must be avoided is reliance solely upon the most uncharitable interpretations of certain positions. Invariably assuming the worst will ensure the perpetration of serious injustice not only towards those with whom one disagrees but also towards oneself, since one may well fail to understand one's own position less well. Rather than argue that as a matter of principle we must either give the most, or the least, charitable reading of a position, what we will say is that the most important thing is to compare like with like: a basic requirement for any comparison, but one frequently left unsatisfied. As far as the comparison of sociological approaches goes, it is important to be equally generous, or stingy, with all points of view, including one's own. To resist, in other words, the natural inclination to be stingy with others and generous to a fault with oneself. Doing this will, as we have pointed out before, make matters much harder because there will be less to choose from. Equally generous treatment to Marx and Weber makes it apparent that the differences between them are much less significant than often alleged. The issue which divides them, whether or not there is any necessity to the pattern of history, is not the kind of thing which can be determined empirically, but is a matter of opting for different assumptions.

However, seeing the choice, as in the case of Marx and Weber, as a matter of assumptions and the preferences they reflect, does not mean that the business comes down to 'you say one thing, I say another'. It is not a matter of whim. What it does mean is that assumptions can be approached from a heuristic point of view, that is, judging them in terms of their value in helping us to make investigations. And, in this respect, either Marx or Weber would do equally well; there is no need to choose between them. In some situations the Marxian assumptions might be the more revealing while in others the Weberian. What we do not have to do is buy either as an exclusive basis of inquiry.

In comparing sociological theories, then, the maxim should be like against like. In addition, a theory should not be criticised for failings which are generic to the discipline. Parsons, for example, is often criticised because his theory is not so much a theory as a collection of categories. It is merely, so it is said, a conceptual scheme, a way of classifying things into an orderly arrangement rather than a set of propositions which say something true or false about the social world. However, if this is true of Parsons' theory, then it is true of most of its rivals. The work of sociology does more often consist in classifications rather than propositions, and even those theories which do approximate to propositional form do not notably perform better than Parsons since they are often empty of significance.

A similar point can be made about the Functionalist argument as we reviewed it in Chapter 2. It is hard to identify functions, but this does not mean that functional explanation is thereby weaker than causal explanation. If it is hard to identify, with confidence, a function, this is because it is hard to make sound empirical judgements of any kind. It is no less difficult in empirical work to identify a cause, or an interest, than it is to locate a function. These sorts of problems are not intrinsic to different theoretical approaches but generic to empirical work in the discipline.

But, if it is important to identify those faults which are generic, it is also important to identify those which are intrinsic to a particular approach, especially from those which are characteristic of a particular interpretation of an approach. This, again, is not an uncommon difficulty in sociologial criticism. Particular interpretations are seized upon and treated as if they were authoritative accounts of the positions to which they are attached and adequate bases for understanding and finding fault. Little effort is made to see if it is necessary to interpret the positions in the way that they are, or to find out if they could be interpreted differently to see if the weaknesses they expose are inevitable ones, or the result of the interpretation itself. The lesson is that it is incumbent on the critic not only to compare like with like and to ensure that equivalently strong accounts are given of the alternatives, it may also be necessary for the critic to give the strongest possible account of the opposition; stronger, perhaps, than even its proponents have managed. If, for example, Weber is to be criticised for idealism, assuming that this is a fault to be avoided, then the critic might first attempt an interpretation of Weber's work which would see to what extent the idealism is necessary. Weber might have been an idealist, but it might turn out that this is not indispensable to his work.

The dispute between sociological approaches is not just about their theories. Sociological approaches also consist of 'metatheoretical' elements; that is, ideas about, among others, the nature and role of theory itself. Long before sociologists of different persuasions start to differ over particular theories they will, likely as not, have parted company on their ideas about what theory should be, what tasks it should fulfil, what problems it should solve, what tests should be applied, and more. There is very little common ground among the various sociological approaches and it is this which makes the exchange of rational criticism so difficult. At no point, or at least rarely, is the disagreement set against a background of agreement. Invariably it is a dispute in which disagreement involves a host of matters both great and small. Criticising one particular approach from the point of view of another comes, as we have said, to reaffirming the differences between them, showing that the parties have very different ideas about sociology. What it does not do is establish that one party is right and the other wrong, only that they see matters differently. This means that the most telling kind of criticism in sociology is likely to be an immanent rather than external criticism which works from within a point of view trying to show that, by its own standards, it leaves much to be desired.

Finally, we may have inadvertently given the impression that evaluating theories and approaches in sociology is a matter of assessing the arguments and presuppositions rather than testing them against empirical evidence: an impression no doubt reinforced by the stress we have laid, in this chapter and Chapter 2 on interpreting theories and the difficulties involved in measuring them against the world. But this is our point. Evaluating theories against the evidence, so to speak, is an important element but among others, and only works to the extent that other tasks have been completed to the best of our abilities. In Chapter 6 we will deal with this matter in more detail. In Chapter 4 we continue our discussion of theorising, this time focusing on the choices available to a sociological theorist in the construction of theories.

FURTHER READING

T B BOTTOMORE and M RUBEL (eds), *Karl Marx: Selected Writings in Sociology and Social Philosophy*, Penguin, 1963. Still useful for the introduction and a wide selection of readings from Marx.

D DAVIDSON, *Inquiries into Truth and Interpretation*, Clarendon, 1984. Contains a full discussion of the principle of charity in connection with problems arising from translation between languages. Our use of it is, of course, much simplified.

H H GERTH and C W MILLS (eds), *From Max Weber: Essays in Sociology*, Routledge, 1967. Contains a good selection of Weber's writings.

Z A JORDAN, *Karl Marx: Economy, Class and Social Revolution*, Michael Joseph, 1971. Contains a long and informative introduction to Marx's thought.

C TAYLOR, *Hegel and Modern Society*, Cambridge University Press, 1979. A brief introduction to Hegel's thought. As ever, Hegel remains difficult.

M WEBER, *The Theory of Social and Economic Organisation*, Oxford University Press, 1947. For an extensive exposition of Weber's ideas. *The Protestant Ethic and the Spirit of Capitalism*, Allen and Unwin, 1965. His statement on the relationship between ascetic Protestantism and the origins of capitalism.

Chapter 4

THEORISING IN SOCIOLOGY

Thus far we have been dealing with the comparison of theories in a general way. We have advocated a policy of tolerance and charity in the interpretation of points of view. We want now to recommend in the evaluation of theories, a sensitivity to the tasks set by the theorist, the goals aspired to and the choices made in trying to meet these goals. In this chapter we will go back to our analogy of games and use it to provide us with a key idea, that of theorising as an activity governed by self-imposed constraints and choices. Theories are selective; they involve opportunity costs in which some aspirations have to be forgone in order to achieve other priorities. Such choices, we want to say, are governed by the ground rules of the game being played. If you are playing golf you cannot knock your opponent's ball out of the way. If you are playing croquet you can. We will follow through some of the self-imposed constraints which can be seen in standard and classical sociology. We hope that a sensitivity to these self-imposed constraints, alongside tolerance and charity, will help to make sociology a more reasoned and intelligible activity than, at times, it appears to be.

One of the more salient features of sociology, as we have noted before, is the way in which it keeps going back to its founding fathers. Even after a century or more of work, we are still bringing the discipline and its topics back to the writings of Marx, Weber, Durkheim, and others. In fact, for many introductory courses, sociology might as well be identified with the writings of these three thinkers. Compared with the natural sciences, progress in sociology is positively glacial. Who would dare, in physics for example, to use Newton's *Opticks*, or in biology, *The Origin of Species*, as first-year texts to be studied in depth and extensively discussed in seminars? Previously, we have made one or two suggestions to account for this apparent lack of progress. More importantly, we have drawn some conclusions about the nature of the discipline from it. Many would argue that one of the reasons for this lack of progress is the fact that sociological theories have a tendency to become detached from reality, so much so that they move beyond test and validation. They fail adequately to circumscribe the phenomena to which they are relevant and hence fail to mesh with one another. In consequence, so this view holds, the discipline consists of an irreducible confusion of irreconcilable theories. We are not sure whether sociology has to be this way. Certainly we do not know of any sensible way of tidying up the discipline. All we hope to do, as we have said all along, is to try to reduce the confusion by, in this chapter, offering some guidelines for discriminating among and understanding various types of theories and the work they do. So, in this chapter we want to talk about theories less as approaches to the discipline and more as instruments, as devices which do a particular kind of work or, to return to the game metaphor, play a particular part in sociology 'games'. It is the self-imposed limitations which, for us, make up the ground rules of sociology 'games'. In this chapter we will make use of this idea to indicate something of the rationale to and sense of the disparate, and often disputing, forms of theorising to be found within the discipline. We shall try to indicate what is involved in striving to obtain different theoretical goals and, in particular, how the pursuit of these goals leads to very different kinds of theorising.

SOCIOLOGY GAMES AND THEORETICAL ACTIVITY

Like all games, sociology 'games' are directed towards ends; they have a point to them. Within our metaphor, this is the equivalent of stating, say, what the aim of soccer is, namely trying to score more goals than the opposing team or, for chess, checkmating the opponent's king. Of course, sociology 'games' are not about winning in quite this sense, nevertheless the analogy is fair enough. It is the game rules which state the contraints which must be observed in trying to achieve these ends; the ends given, as it were, within the game itself. While there may be many reasons we could offer for playing soccer, chess, solitaire, and sociology, these do not determine what the aim of the game is as far as its playing is concerned. They do not, to put it another way, determine the point of the game. What we are saying here is that sociology 'games' are directed towards some recognisably sociological end. The personal and other reasons which lead a sociologist to be interested in a particular problem, or indeed in the discipline itself, are irrelevant to how the game is to be played, how the stated ends are to be achieved. How any scientist or scholar arrives at his or her ideas, whether in the bath, being hit on the head with an apple, listening to Jackson Brown, is an entirely separate matter from how the ideas are supported, the theories confirmed, warranted, and grounded: in short, how the game is played.

Further, playing sociology 'games' is to take a special sort of interest in the world, one which is first and foremost theoretical rather than practical and which tries resolutely to keep practical considerations at arm's length and subordinate to theoretical ones. This is what we meant in Chapter 1 when we talked of the self-sufficiency of games. The interest lies in playing the game, doing the sociology, which may or may not be related to other practical ends or purposes quite independent of the game itself.

We readily accede that this implication from our game analogy is at odds with one conventional view of the nature of sociology. Sociology does have a lot to say about educational inequality, poverty, crime and deviance, power, and other problems. And what it has to say about them looks to have practical import, with many of its theories being directed to the remedy or amelioration of such problems. Indeed, it is quite apparent that a reforming impulse did motivate much of early sociological endeavour and continues to do so. But we think it is important to notice that such theories *are* theories, that is the product of reflection upon the social world which have *then* been put to particular use. In theoretical reflections in sociology, phenomena are characterised in *sociological ways*, that is by means of sociological concepts and with sociological interests in mind. One of these, of course, may very well be the eventual formulation of a public policy or some other remedy. But it does not have to be. The activity of theorising is not necessarily tied to practical concerns, but the latter cannot proceed without the former; that is, the practical application of sociology cannot be divorced from theorising. So, although sociology does indeed offer solutions to poverty, inequality, and so forth, it begins by treating these as sociologically defined problems, and therefore arrives at views of them which may or may not coincide with those generally held by ordinary members of society.

This idea is not an easy one to grasp. Debates over what it involves are continuing in the discipline. Fortunately, for our purposes, we do not have to do more than mark the distinction between theorising and the practical application of theories. We do not have to bring the debate to a conclusion. What we will be concerned with is theorising as a self-contained activity. Whatever else it might be, whatever arguments might be raised about the uses to which it should be put and the topics it should deal with are not our immediate concern.

To repeat, sociology 'games' are directed to some recognisably sociological end. Each game, as it were, defines its own moves, its own pieces, sets its own problems to solve, and, equally important, offers its own criteria of success and failure. In this way, using the game analogy, we can begin to look at sociological theories in the way recommended in the conclusion to Chapter 3, that is, from *within*.

Let us take the analogy a little further. Just as we can see the actions of soccer players as directed towards scoring goals and preventing goals being scored against them, within the game itself there are many problems which have to be solved in order to achieve the overall end. The ball has to be won, opponents tackled, passes made accurately, space created, opposing players drawn out of position, and so on. Similarly, in chess, checkmating the opponent's king is the end product of facing and solving problems that arise throughout the game itself. Of course, the kinds of problem that arise depend upon the game being played and the resources needed to cope with them. So it is with sociology 'games'.

THE PROBLEM-SOLVING NATURE OF THEORY

Highlighting the problem-solving nature of theoretical activity is intended to de-emphasise some of the prevailing doctrines students receive in discussions of the philosophy of science as it allegedly applies to the social sciences. As we suggested earlier in our discussion of the relation between sociology and philosophy, as far as we are concerned, a more useful way of looking at scientific practice is to see it as problem-solving activity, and theories important because they provide *more or less* satisfactory ways of solving scientific problems by reducing ambiguity, producing patterns out of seeming irregularity, and showing that what happens is intelligible and predictable.

Of course, scientific problems do not just appear. They are not just given in the world as intrinsically puzzling bits of data or facts, although the world, however we choose to characterise it, is their origin. Problems of the kind we are talking about arise within the particular context of an inquiry and, accordingly, depend in some large part on the theories and ideas we possess at the time. So, if the solving of sociological problems is the motivational impulse behind sociological activity, theories are the end product. They are the solutions to such problems and, we must add, an important source of other problems.

Scientific problems are not all of a piece. Empirical problems are, perhaps, the kind we normally associate with the idea of problems;

that is, substantive questions that arise about the objects constituted by a given discipline. Why do heavy bodies fall to the ground when unsupported? Why do prices rise? Why does a lot of beer make you drunk? Why do people commit crime? These are empirical problems in this sense, and many of them also puzzles and problems which arise in the ordinary world. None the less, the problems that concern us always arise within a domain of inquiry and are, thereby, in large part defined by the context. It is our theoretical presuppositions which tell us what to expect and which shape, what is peculiar, puzzling, and questionable. For example, working-class Conservative voters in Britain are a puzzle only within the context of inquiry which sees this as a problem, namely a group who according to the 'theories' are doing something odd, that is, voting for a party which does not represent their political interests. They are not a problem, at least in this immediate sense, to party election managers, to themselves, nor for theories of voting which do not place class membership as the prime determinant of political action. We should also point out that it is not always clear whether a problem is a genuine one or not, to which set of theories it rightfully belongs, nor even which discipline is its proper home. Yet again, these matters for argument and inquiry. Further, the solutions to problems are always approximate and temporary, always a matter of judgement and debate.

Perhaps the most important problems a discipline has to face are conceptual, although the distinction between these and empirical ones is not always clear-cut; they are problems encountered within theories themselves. These can be ambiguities and circularities within the theories, difficulties over reconciling one theory with another, and many more. An important source of such problems in the history of the natural sciences, and the social sciences are no different in this respect, are cases where theories from one domain of inquiry conflict with those from another, as is sometimes claimed about sociological theories and those from sociobiology, or between Freudian theories and social learning theories in psychology. Alternatively, theories may have different methodological prescriptions as, for example, those based on the use of official statistics compared with other theories about the social production of such statistics. Sometimes, of course, a theory may clash with a prevailing world view, as Marxist sociology does, at least in the West. In none of these cases are such problems easy to resolve. Indeed, one should say that it is the attempt at solution which constitutes the theoretical life of the discipline.

CRITERIA FOR EVALUATING THEORIES

The aim of theory, then, is to solve problems; theories are the end product of a problem-solving process. Within this, however, particular kinds of theories have their own aims and pursuits which, and this is very important, have their own criteria for evaluation. In other words, the criteria involved in weighing, judging, and indeed constructing theories are more than simply that the theory is correct, that it is confirmed by the facts, and so on. After all, scoring goals is the point of football and whether the ball is scrambled over the line or cannoned in with a beautiful left-foot shot, the goal still counts; the problem has been solved. Yet, there is still a significant sense in which we might concern ourselves with how well the goal was scored, with a left-foot drive rather than the messy scramble. We might well be concerned, to put it another way, with how we go about the business of solving problems. For example, in the natural and mathematical sciences it is usual to judge theories against a number of standards including generality, simplicity, parsimony, elegance, consistency, and operationality. These standards can be seen as a set of preferences where it is usual to prefer a more general theory to one that is less general, one that is simpler over one that is more complex, and so on, providing of course that the theory does actually solve the problem in hand, or is a reasonable step towards a solution. Such standards are not absolutes which have to be attained at all costs, but represent judgements with regard to what is currently on view in the discipline concerned. Just as problem-solving is a relative matter, so a theory is preferred, given that it offers a solution to the problem, to the extent that it is more general, elegant, simpler, and so on than another. Nor are these criteria absolutes across disciplines. Theories in mathematics, for example, may be more elegant and more internally consistent than those in biology, although they may not be as empirically applicable. Neither of these facts makes them better or worse theories. While acknowledging this, however, it is the case that the best scientific theories do appear to be preferable to their competitors on many if not all of the criteria mentioned. Other, less prestigious but none the less perfectly usable theories may not be.

In the social sciences, matters are not quite so straightforward. In sociology certainly, there is little evidence that theories even attempt to meet the classical canons for theorising just mentioned. Nor, as we have seen, is there very much sense of a steady accumulation of theories and findings of the sort that we do find in disciplines against which sociology tends to measure itself. Sociology has, of course, made 'progress' but, all too often, this goes unrecognised since much of the dissatisfaction with its theories arises from the adoption of inappropriate or less useful criteria for what constitutes theoretical progress. To explain this a little more clearly, let us go back to the distinction made in Chapter 2 between the 'internalist' and the 'externalist' views of theory.

In Chapter 2 we suggested that externalists argue that the world, or reality if you prefer, consists of mind-independent objects and it is the aim of science to provide us with true descriptions of these objects and the relations between them. It is this posture that enables us to speak of the *discovery* of DNA or Pluto and not of their invention. The overriding implication is that eventually it will be possible to give one, complete, exhaustive, and true description of how things are in the external world. This, it is readily acceded, will be a long and arduous business, nevertheless one important measure of scientific progress is the growing and cumulative body of theories which offer better and better descriptions of external reality. Internalists, on the other hand, while not denying the existence of the external world, wonder if 'fitting' theories and the world is quite as straightforward a matter as externalists are prone to claim. Methods of measurement, an important way of connecting theories with the world, are always dependent upon some theory which says, at the very least, how some objects are to be measured. So, in effect, it is theories which tell us what is to count as a good fit with reality and what is not, and hence there is no theory-independent way of assessing how well a theory describes the world. As a result, the internalist is much more concerned to ask what kinds of theoretical descriptions can be given of the objects in the world than what the world is like independent of our theories of it. As far as progress in science is concerned, rather than emphasising its cumulative nature, the internalist lays greater stress on theoretical innovation itself, its newsworthiness, its ability to identify researchable problems, and so on.

In our earlier discussion, we were at pains to point out that the choice between the internalist and the externalist accounts of theory was an open one, and that by recommending an internalist stance we do not mean that one is free to dream up theories at will. One cannot adopt just any framework one wishes, or do whatever one likes within a framework. Each has its own limitations and requirements not by any means realised at first glance, and, above all, each is constrained by how things actually are.

Much theoretical work in sociology looks and sounds as if it is being carried on under the externalist rubric. While this is not wrong, we have insisted that these matters are arguable after all – it is, we think, one source of the dissatisfaction often voiced in and about sociology. Accordingly, we suggest, if only for strategic reasons, finding one's way around theories in sociology might be more easily achieved by seeing them as expressions of an internalist stance whether or not they are explicitly so. This is not, let us hasten to add, a prescription for ending the debate between internalists and externalists, for that is a long way off, but a proposal for how we might begin to grasp some of the issues at stake in the construction of sociological theories. Here we want to exploit the internalist stance for heuristic reasons, as a way of thinking about theorising in sociology or, to use the game metaphor, thinking about the ways in which sociology 'games' play with theories. The main advantage of the internalist stance, at least as we see it, is that although the world as it actually is, is important for the truth of a theory, great variety in theorising is made possible. It encourages us to look at theories in their own terms as alternative ways of going about understanding the world sociologically. It also means that we do not need to be inhibited immediately by questions concerning how a theory is supposed to match reality but can talk, very conveniently, of reality-in-the-theory. It allows us to talk of theories, and this perhaps is the point of our game metaphor, as if they were different forms of playing with ideas rather than the single-minded determination to produce one, true description of how things are. So, on this view, one of the major aims of theorising will be to follow through ideas, analogies, idealisations, etc. to their descriptive conclusion in constituting limited aspects of the world, *whatever* this may turn out to be like.

CHOICES IN THEORY CONSTRUCTION

Sociology exhibits great variety in its forms of theorising, something that we would, incidently, expect if its theorising were done under the internalist rubric. We will try to preserve and present this variety by talking about theory and theorising as involving explicit choices concerning the aims of a theory, its form, the standards it will aspire to meet, and so on. In what follows, we will outline some of the main dimensions along which these choices are made. We stress that we are electing to illuminate sociological theorising as choices exercised by the theorist and not claiming for a moment that theorists explicitly have these in mind when designing their theories. Nevertheless, treating theories as the deliberate result of exercising options means that we *have* to view them as reasoned and calculated and not as the expression of blind prejudice, whimsy, or simple stupidity. As we have emphasised before, sociology ought to be a reasoned pursuit and treating it as if it were means that we might see more sense in some of the things which, at first glance, we find puzzling or outrageous.

In the following discussion we express the play of theoretical ideas as a set of dichotomous choices. Our list is not definitive nor exhaustive. Nor is it our desire to force every theory in sociology into this framework. The frame is intended as a way of understanding sociological theorising as a reasoned activity so that, hopefully, it will prove a great deal less mystifying and, dare we say it, irritating. We express the choices in dichotomous fashion to stress the fact that while theorising in one way might have advantages, it also has its costs, though neither are always immediately apparent. However, expressing the choices as either/or is somewhat unrealistic and a number of them should be regarded as involving more of this and less of that: continua in other words.

The choices we shall discuss are as follows:
1. Ethical commitment and value neutrality.
2. Realism and conventionalism.
3. Positivist and Interpretativist research implications.
4. Empirical and theoretical goals of concept formation.
5. Maximising and minimising constraints of theory.

Sociological theories, then, can be thought of as the outcomes of the theorist exercising options with regard to some or all of these choices. As we proceed with the discussion, it will become apparent that there are important connections between some of these choices in the sense that a particular choice on one will have influence on or implications for choices on others. Theories will seem, that is, to cluster. However, our aim is not to produce a classification of types of theory, but to present a way of looking at theorising as an activity, explicating the kinds of reasons that theorists have for moving in the directions they do.

Ethical commitment and value neutrality

What is involved here, and it is an issue which surfaces in a number of ways, is whether a theorist should have a clear idea of just what outcomes or uses a theory might have in advance of the theory's development. One could say here that the choice is between whether theorising should be directed towards some purpose or controlled by its relevance to some project. Put this way, this is not a matter, as is usually supposed, of whether or not sociology can divest itself of ethical, moral, and political concerns, but whether it should be in the service of arguments over these things. It will surely come as no surprise that sociologists differ on this as on other matters; there is, in other words, a choice here. It is a difference of view which has been with sociology since its inception. Weber, for example, was harshly critical of those who wished to subordinate their academic work to their political and moral values and hence used their academic positions to disseminate moral and political opinions. For Weber, scientific work ought to be value-neutral. While cultural values might dictate the kinds of problems a scientist wishes to investigate, these should not enter into the investigtion, the science itself.

Marx, for one, would not have agreed with Weber. For Marx, the accepted ideas in a society are those which support the position of the dominant class. Accordingly, the producers of ideas, mainly but not only academics, either support these ideas or try to expose them as ideologies, as ideas tied to the interests of a particular group. There is no neutral ground. The producers of ideas must commit themselves to one side or the other. As far as he himself was concerned, Marx's ideas are directed towards hastening the overthrow of the capitalist system, and so his theories are intendedly revolutionary.

In both the case of Marx and that of Weber, their attitude on this issue, while consonant with their styles of sociological theorising, is an attitude brought to that work and not a product of it. It does not matter whether one prefers Marx's position to that of Weber, or whether one wishes to adopt another one altogether, so long as we notice that the choice here involves a commitment. For Weber it was a commitment to non-partisan sociology; for Marx it was a commitment to a revolutionary ideology and hence to critical sociology. For Weber, the task was, as far as possible, to distance oneself from one's moral and political preferences in sociology. For Marx, the point was to engage them.

It is also equally important to note that sociology itself cannot prescribe which of these two predispositions should prevail. The choice cannot be made through sociological reasoning. Yet, though outside the bounds of sociology, the choice crucially affects what goes on in the discipline; what kind of phenomena are investigated, what kind of topics a theorist might deal with, and so on. Thus, although Weber stressed that sociology should be value-neutral in the contruction of its theories, wider cultural concerns may guide and shape theorising. His own interests, for example, in rationality, in bureaucracy, forms of authority, were explicitly guided by a concern with what was going on in Western European societies at the time. But, whatever else the connections are between an ethical commitment and the sociological theories a theorist espouses, they are not logical entailments. Sociologists do not argue their way from moral preferences to sociological theories, or vice versa. Rather, the commitments serve to rationalise the choices within the theories. Decisions to set out a theory in a particular way, or to move in a particular direction with a theory, may be made precisely because it is possible to see what the outcomes will be and to what uses it will be put.

There is another matter here worth mentioning that has to do with the evaluation of theory. To reject a theory simply because it expresses a set of ethical or political commitments is tantamount to saying no more than 'I would not do it this way', which may be true but irrelevant, sociologically speaking. There have been occasions, for example, when sociology has been condemned because, and only because, it is Marxist or Marxist inspired. In other words, because it has been seen as espousing or reflecting a particular set of moral values. Whether or not sociology is, or was, Marxist inspired, or whether Marxism is anti-democratic, or whatever, is all beside the point in the judgement of the intellectual worth of a discipline. Though, of course, they may be relevant in other contexts. Nor is it only non-sociologists who are guilty of this kind of condemnation. Sociologists, too, have done their share. Our point is that the criticism of moral and political commitments is likely to be more effective, again sociologically speaking, when it sets out to demonstrate that the adoption of different moral choices would have made significant differences to the theory in question. After all, it does not follow that Marx's theory is wrong simply by virtue of the political goals to which he subscribed, or right either. Neither, to take a more contemporary case from another discipline, can we say that merely because Milton Friedman wants the absolute minimum of state intervention in social life, his monetarist theories must be wrong. Both Marx and Friedman might be wrong, or right, but not because of the political commitments they bring to their theories. Such commitments may, indeed, affect theories but this needs to be shown and not assumed. Some of the more strident criticism of Marxist sociology, for example, would be improved if, instead of decrying it because of its evaluative stance towards the processes of capitalist accumulation, it were to work out in detail what the consequences for the theory might be if such a moral evaluation were to be abandoned. Would it make any difference to the theory as a theory? Would it still be able to meet the goals set for it, and so on?

Realism and conventionalism

The choice here is a particularly acute one for sociology, and has to do with how far sociological theories should portray the ordinary world as experienced by the people who live in it. One of the bewilderments which afflicts many students in their first engagement with the discipline is that though, ostensibly, it is about the study of human social life, it does not portray people as they are 'ordinarily experienced'. There is often a surrealist air about sociological conceptions of social actors. 'People just aren't like that!' is the exasperated cry.

Clearly there is a great deal involved here. For one thing, this worry exhibits a confusion over the nature of theoretic disciplines and what it is they set out to do, as well as the limitations they accept. Nevertheless, some of the confusion may be reduced if we try to look at this matter through the choices that a theoretician is free to exercise in connecting a theory to the social world. Given the stance we discussed at the beginning, there is no necessary reason why a sociological theory should, to put it this way, mirror the social world-as-experienced-by-ordinary-people. A theory may choose to portray the world as one recognisable to the persons who live within it, so to speak, or it may set itself other aims in which this particular aspiration is not paramount. This is what we mean here as a choice between 'realism' and 'conventionalism'.

Look at it this way. On the one hand we have the ordinary social world and, on the other some sociological theory about it, or about part of it. A 'realist' would want to ensure that theory preserved the essential characteristics of that social world in order to underpin the plausibility of the theory. We would expect the theory to present the ordinary world in a way which corresponded, in large measure, with how ordinary people encountered it. The world pictured in the theory would have to be recognisably the world in which ordinary people lived. For the 'conventionalist', however, the immediate recognisability of a theory is not a primary aim. Instead, such a theorist aims to produce a particular picture of the world in order to bring out certain features. He would be more concerned with the conventions of a way of picturing than with attaining a correspondence with what is ordinarily recognisable. We can illustrate this difference by talking about maps.

As a method of expressing relationships, there are no immutable constraints on how maps must be drawn. As long as a map succeeds in expressing the relationships it is designed to, it will be successful and acceptable. For example, a map of the London Underground might be designed so that it preserved as many of the geographical features of the system, the distance between stations, the compass bearing of the lines relative to one another, the depths of the lines below the surface, and so on. It might do this, but there is no requirement that it should. Indeed, the familiar dendritic maps found on all Underground stations preserve only two features; the distinctions between the lines, which are picked out in different colours, and the succession of the stations on them. Of course, one cannot use these maps to determine how far apart the stations are, nor in what direction one would have to walk or drive from one to another by surface routes. One could, of course, make the map more 'realistic' by marking in all the buildings, roads, relative positions, and the rest, but for its purpose the map does not need any of these.

There are, naturally, 'realist' and 'conventionalist' elements in all theories, so practically speaking what we have here is a choice between theoretical priorities; between a choice which stresses the predominance of the recognisability of the social world in the theory, and another which is much more interested in, so to speak, the arts of theorising themselves. Both have to make contact with, must relate to, the social world, but how and in what fashion is a matter of theoretical priorities.

The contrast involved here, and the choice it represents, can be seen in the comparison between, say, Oscar Lewis' study of a Puerto Rican family in San Juan and New York, which illustrates the 'culture of poverty theory' and Marx's treatment of, among other things, the causes of poverty in capitalist society. We must be careful here. We are using this comparison to illuminate different theoretical styles and not implying that Lewis and Marx have alternative theories of poverty. They may or may not have, that is not our concern. Lewis' interest is in exploring how poverty as a way of life is passed down from generation to generation. It is a culture of coping; coping with the helplessness and despair which stem from the impossibility of achieving success in the wider society. His way of presenting his theory is through a detailed account of the experiences of members of the Puerto Rican family, and his narrative, often presented in the words of the people themselves, is full of all the life, views, hopes, opinions, and fears that we recognise ordinary human beings, whether Puerto Rican or not, have. Marx's aim, on the other hand, is to explain poverty as the outcome of deep processes at work in the political economy of capitalism; processes which are emphatically not directly apprehended by ordinary people and which do not operate at this level of social reality. Social actors are the instruments of forces shaped and forged by the logic of the capitalist economy. Marx's theoretical aspirations do not require him to present a 'realistic' portrayal of life in society, though he often does so, in the way that Lewis does of the culture of poverty. Marx's task is to unearth the forces which explain, among other things, why some people are poor and why a minority are rich. To achieve this, he does not need to offer a 'realistic' picture of what it is like to be poor, or rich.

What it is important to notice here is how implausible it is to suggest that Lewis and Marx are offering competing theories of 'the facts'. What they choose to describe and the ways they choose to describe it are entirely different. Lewis wants a theory which expresses how poor people experience and reproduce their poverty. Marx wants a social theory which shows how certain orders of class relations require it.

This distinction between 'realism' and 'conventionalism' is obviously methodological in character, as are the other distinctions set out in this chapter. That is to say, we are not implying that 'realism' is better or worse than 'conventionalism', simply that any evaluation depends on the theoretical goals we wish to achieve. As ways of mapping the world, all theories are selective, abstracting out some features rather than others. However, having said this, it is all too easy to fall into the temptation which we discussed in Chapter 2 and convert it into a metaphysical matter by insisting that what we ought to ask is what the *real causes* of poverty are, to stay with the example we were using, and hence to end up once again with the dispute between the externalists and the internalists. We think it would be as well to avoid this by giving up any metaphysical ambitions for theories, and as we said before deliberately turning away from looking for a fit between the theory and reality, and instead talking of reality-in-the-theory. Although this is difficult to do, let alone sustain, it does push the requirements of sociological theorising to a central position rather than squeezing them out by an overconcentration on metaphysical and other philosophical problems. It also avoids the all too easy identification of social reality with some notion of reality as ordinarily experienced, whatever that means. All theories abstract, even extremely 'realist' ones, and there is no necessity that the social reality in the theory should be that ordinarily encountered. In other words, it is no attack upon a sociological theory that it fails to capture the ordinary world as we know it, if this is not its aim.

Having said this, though, there is a widespread and natural tendency to 'read into' theories elements from ordinary experience, either by way of refutation or to make them more plausible and understandable. Something of what is at stake here can be seen in the way that Marx's conception of the nature of social class is understood. The 'working class' is not only a sociological category, it is a lay one too. Moreover, it is a category used in a variety of sociological theories and does not always have the same meaning. For Marx, 'the working class' is defined as a group created by the labour processes of capitalism and having a special relationship to the process of capital accumulation and the expropriation of surplus value. It is not, in other words, a category which is coterminal with what, commonsensically, we might understand the working class to be. It is arguable, for instance, that university lecturers and teachers are working class in the Marxist sense, though they are hardly that to most people who work in manual occupations. But this is no objection to Marx's theory, though it might be to the expression which he has chosen. We need to give close attention to the 'conventional' element in his work rather than treating it as an exercise in 'realism'. Seeing it in this way, enables us to judge just what is required by way of investigating his ideas, how well Marx satisfies his own theoretical aims, and what would be required to connect it to the world.

Positivist and Interpretivist research implications.

Although, in a later chapter, we shall deal more fully with the question of whether sociology can aspire to be a science or not, this dichotomy is an aspect of that discussion. One of the purposes of theory is to guide research. Theory tells us what has to be investigated in order to bring out a solution to a problem, be it empirical or conceptual. Theory tells us what data are relevant, and in this sense what sort of 'stuff' is to count as data. As far as sociology is concerned, this determining role is often represented in the choice between Positivist and Interpretivist research implications. The former takes the view that, to all intents and purposes, social life can be treated as if it were a species of natural life; that is, to be investigated using the methods and logic derived from the natural sciences. The Interpretivists tend to deny this. For them, there is a qualitative difference between social phenomena and natural phenomena which must needs be reflected in the methods used in research. Thus the Positivist looks to construct theory which is formalised, quantifiable, consisting of explanatory generalisations and containing precisely defined variables. Interpretivists, on the other hand, are less enamoured of these aspirations and prefer to collect material which delineates the meanings which courses of action have for those who engage in them, and are less interested in being able to formulate explanatory mechanisms.

One of the salient differences between these two stances, and we shall have more to say about this in Chapter 6, is the different role which they allocate to theory. For the Positivist, the point of theory is to allow for explanation based upon generalisation, which in turn must be testable. If an explanation survives such tests, then the theory works and can be accommodated within the corpus of theoretical knowledge for the time being at least. Testing is not the only criterion that a theory has to meet, but it is a crucial one. For the interpretivists, the point of theory is to sensitise the investigator to the reasons, views, aspirations, motives, and perceptions that lie behind what social actors do. Consequently, the setting of test conditions and the extraction of generalisations are not paramount. The theory works to the extent that it does sensitise the research and enables the understanding of the phenomena being investigated.

Once again we are concerned with styles of theorising which cannot be ranked in any absolute sense. However, having opted for one, it is difficult to retain the advantages of the other. Such choices involve 'opportunity costs'. There have been attempts to synthesise the two styles, but few have been successful since, given the very different role and nature of theory involved in each, it is difficult to see how the advantages of both could be maximised at the same time. This being the case, we have to be especially careful when comparing research done under one option with that done under the other, since there may not be any common standard with which to effect the comparison.

As we mentioned earlier we will be discussing these matters in greater detail in Chapter 6, so we can leave them here for the moment.

Empirical and theoretical goals of concept formation

This dimension concerns how concepts function within a theory. Since theories differ on so much else, it is not surprising that they display deep divergencies over how a theory should be operationalised. This has given rise to considerable confusion. For many, sociology seems to consist of endless discussion of concepts rather than the discovery of facts. Weber's monumental work *Economy and Society*, for example, contains page after page of definition and elaboration of concepts such as 'social action', 'rational action', 'economic action', 'ideal types', 'subjective meaning'. Similarly, Durkheim's empirical study of suicide contains a great deal of conceptual discussion. If we begin with the assumption that the choice to take up conceptual discussion is a reasoned one and not whimsy, its proliferation might indicate its importance for theorising. Although we recog nise that the nature of concepts and their relations to theories involv many complex and multi-faceted matters, we will pull out just one fo our discussion, namely the use of concepts as empirical indicators o as theoretical constructs. This should be enough to indicate the scop and nature of the choices involved.

What we want to draw attention to is the relative degree to whicl theoretical knowledge is felt to be necessary to make observations When we were discussing 'internalism' and 'externalism', we used th example of the observation of particle tracks in high-energy physics More than just a little knowledge is required to be able to see th scrawls and marks *as* particle tracks. Very little theoretica knowledge, though, is needed to see a child's slide as an inclined plan down which bodies of given mass can accelerate at uniform rates. I this latter case, very few of us would have much difficulty makin observation statements, measurements, and so on about clearl existing bodies in motion. We could not say the same thing about th particle tracks. The tracks are being used as a resource to see *if* th particles which have been theorised can be seen. And if they cannot this does not imply that they do not exist or that the theory is wrong but that this method of looking for them has not worked. Those of a empirical cast of mind insist that concepts must be related to ob servable phenomena; others may be quite happy to look for observ ables which just might be instances of the conceptualised object.

Yet again we can see just how easy it is to turn such differences int metaphysical rather than methodological questions. Some forms o empiricism, albeit not quite as fashionable in sociology now as the once were, would deny any sense to concepts which could not b translated into observation statements. Unfortunately, this onl served to remove most of the more interesting concepts the disciplin possessed. The point is that one important aspect of theorising i connecting together concepts *within* the theory so that it might prov successful in investigation either as a possible generalisation or as sensitising framework. Empirical work is difficult enough, an without concepts to guide it, it is hard to see how it could be got off th ground at all.

Even where there is a determination to operationalise concepts s that they yield observation statements, differences appear. Take th concept of alienation. This can be defined roughly in the followin manner. We can say that individuals may be located in particula social groupings according to the relationship they stand in witl regard to the productive forces in their society. These relations are then, class relations and involve exploitation and oppression. One is either a member of the exploiting and oppressing class, or one is a member of that which is exploited and oppressed. Oppression and exploitation may take many forms. One of these is the 'reification' of creativity and the 'alienation of labour power' to be seen in the loss of control which the labourer experiences over work and its products, the treatment of labour as a commodity to be bought and sold, and with these, its conception in instrumental and dehumanising terms. This formulation of alienation could be operationalised in several ways. We could take clusters of phenomena, say strikes, disputes, restrictive practices, quality control, absenteeism, leisure activities, trade union membership, and the satisfaction derived from work, and treat them as *indicators* of the degree of alienation in different occupational contexts and organisational settings. We might find doctors to be less alienated than factory workers, women in small-scale assembly plants to be less alienated than female teachers in large comprehensive schools, and so on. We could also chart the change over time of levels of alienation in particular industries and occupations. This would give us one way of studying alienation. Equally well, the concept would be operationalised by regarding alienation as an endemic feature of the particular socio-historical context of modern capitalist societies. We could then trace it through the spontaneous emergence of mass movements, revolutionary parties, and the radicalisation of strategic groups such as the intellectual middle classes, the young, and minority ethnic groups, the provision of channels of protest and the legitimation of certain forms of political action, and how all of these were related to the changing nature of productive relations in any society. This would give entirely different types of studies.

Whichever way we wish to express our interest in the concept, the point is that there can never be just one way of operationalising 'alienation' which is the correct one. Operations and measurements belong to theories. What is never to be found is the elaboration of a theoretical scheme and then the hunting around for the best way to proceduralise it, no matter how much it might appear to look like this. Elaboration takes place within the context of a strategy of investigation. The net result is, of course, that theorists appear to be arguing not so much at cross purposes but in entirely different theoretical terms, even though they are employing the same vocabulary. It is for this reason that the interest in theoretical concepts is an important one.

Maximising and minimising constraints of theory

One of the important characteristics that we wanted to derive from the internalist-externalist distinction was the way that it enabled us to capture the range of variation that could be allowed within a theory. We called this 'the play of ideas'. All theories engage in it to some extent, but some carry such variation far beyond where others are willing to go. None, though, are willing to vary everthing at once, for this would be impossible. The choice of what to vary and how far to vary it indicates the range of constraints a theory is responsive to. Maps of the London Underground, you will recall, were constrained only by the distinction of the lines and the order of the stations. Other maps respect other constraints. Applying this to theory, what emerges is the possibility that one of the goals for theorising can become the investigation of just exactly what does follow if particular constraints are held to or suspended. Talking in realist and conventionalist terms for a moment, we might be able to say that if we adopt a conventionalist set of constraints we might be released from the need to theorise social life in ways that match our ordinary experience. Thus we might be free to visualise social life as if it were a beehive or other insect colony, as a set of games, economic exchanges, or even a mechnical system like a car engine. The realist, on the other hand wants to maximise at least one constraint, namely that theory accommodates to the world as that is known or experienced by ordinary people.

This difference is brought out if we think about a familiar example like the formation of condensation on a window. When the temperature outside falls and is lower than the temperature inside, differential vapour pressure occurs each side of the window pane, the pressure inside the room is higher than that outside. This causes the water vapour in the air to try to drive through the glass, but once it contacts the cold surface of the pane it condenses. In this explanation, the only relevant factors are the gaseous properties of water vapour and the cold surface. The thickness of the glass might be relevant, but its opacity would not, nor would whether the window was in the front of the house or in the back, in Dagenham or Dar es Salaam. The relevant constant elements in the theory would be the temperature of the water vapour, the differential vapour pressure, and the relative coldness of the pane of glass. These would appear in any explanation of condensation using this particular theoretical description.

We can use the same idea of making selections and holding different things constant when we turn to sociological theory. For example, take the respective discussions of power offered by C Wright Mills and Talcott Parsons. For Mills what was essential in a power relation was that it was a relation of domination. One party enforced their will at the expense of another. The ability to do this systematically is not evenly distributed in a society but accumulates in particular locations which Mills called 'the command posts'. Mills argued that occupation of these command posts was becoming increasingly homogenous and hence that modern society was evolving a 'power élite'. In theorising power in this way, Mills saw his task as the documentation of this process and the identification of the personnel involved. He wanted to give a clear and recognisable picture of what the distribution of power was really like. Parsons approaches the concept from an entirely different viewpoint. He defines power as a 'medium of exchange' operating rather like the oil in a car engine, or money in an economy, facilitating the smooth running of society. For him, it is the circulation of power which is to be held constant rather than its accumulation. Parsons treats power not as a property of persons but of systems of social relationships. Imbalances in power reflect failures in the circulatory mechanisms, or necessary functions. The hierarchical and dominatory conception of power central to Mills is absent altogether from Parsons. As a consequence, the theoretical descriptions and explanations which are given of the distribution of power in American society or the outburst of McCarthyism in the 1950s differ widely. They differ in their starting-points and what they hold constant. In which case, it makes little or no sense to ask which of them is the more correct. They also reflect how these different choices reflect the choices which sociologists bring to their work. Mills wanted to make the general public aware of what he felt were the increasingly anti-democratic tendencies in American political life as part of his determination to make sociology connect 'public issues' and 'private troubles'. Parsons wanted a systemic conception of power that could be placed within a general social theory.

The choices we have been outlining constitute, for us, some of the main dimensions along which sociological theories differ. In addition, we would like to conclude by mentioning some of the preferences which inform the choices theorists make. Probably the most obvious of these is the general conception of theorising which is adopted. Some theorists, for example, seem to hold to a 'zero-sum' conception of theorising in which alternatives are held to be mutually exclusive and, if a balance of advantage lies with one theory, then a corresponding balance of disadvantage must lie with another or others. For every theoretical 'winner' there must be a theoretical 'loser'. The views held by some 'externalists' of 'internalism' capture this rather nicely. This zero-sum view has one rather unhappy consequence. It leads to a tendency to think that if a particular criticism or evaluation can be sustained for one theory then its obverse or inverse must be true of its competitors. If Marxism is materialist, then its competitors must be idealist, if Functionalism is objective then Interactionism must be subjective. But it is not the case that integral to every theory is an immanent critique of all of its rivals.

The zero-sum conception does have its uses though. It is a good way of marking out the differences between the claims that theories can make and a useful aid to innovative theorising. It also emphasises the internal strengths of theories, the goals they set, the clarity of their concepts, but it also forces choices on an all or nothing basis; a conception which does not square with the pluralist view of the discipline we have been describing and advocating.

A second preference some theorists have is a willingness to take risks. One way that this can be done is to make precise predictions which might be used as tests of validity. A second way of taking risks is to look for a theory that is more general than its competitors, one which collects together more phenomena including those its competitors deal with. A good example of this is Einstein's theory of relativity, which accounts for all of the phenomena which Newton's theory does, and then some of those where Newton's failed. In sociology, Durkheim's theory of anomie has proven generalisable across the range of deviance. It is hard to imagine how 'differential association' theory might be.

The riskiness of a theory is not the same thing as a theory springing surprises, although it can involve this. Einstein, for example, began with relativity and found himself, very unwillingly, in quantum mechanics. He was never quite able to reconcile himself to the indeterminacy which his theories were found to imply. In sociology the range of risks to be run can be seen in the various syntheses that have been offered of macro- and microsociology. Some, wishing to minimise the drawbacks supposedly associated with either side have offered bland amalgams of various sorts. Others, such as George Homans, have tried for synthesis by going out on a limb. For our immediate purposes, it does not matter whether we agree with Homans or not that all human behaviour is explicable by reference to the psychology of personal decision-making construed in stimulus/response/reinforcement terms. What is relevant is that it is a challenging and risky theory which sets itself against the usual sociological preconceptions. If Homans could sustain his case then he would be laying the foundations of a very different kind of sociology, while the versions which run fewer risks would make little or no difference to how things are in the discipline. For them, partial success is better than outright failure.

Connected to this preference for risk, is our final preference. If we think of theories as designed to solve problems or overcome difficulties, then some will attack a greater array than others. Some, like our condensation example, may be so limited to be hardly interesting at all. Others may be significant only because they aim to be general. The range is well illustrated by the contrast between Crick and Watson's discovery of the structure of DNA and functional theories in sociology. The constraints upon the structure of DNA were what was already known about the protein and the work that it did in genetic processes. Not just any structure would fit the bill. The double helix satisfied the requirements. In functional accounts of social phenomena, on the other hand, it is very difficult at times to tell whether the proposed functional connections between conditions and consequences do, in fact, account for any phenomenon's existence. The difficulty seems to be avoided by a presumption that if a phenomenon exists there must be some identifiable function for it to perform. The maxim which functional descriptions follow appears to be something like this: 'Here are some more as yet unacknowledged advantages accruing from. . .'. The functional explanation satisfies just one small cluster of difficulties in providing a logic to social activities. The double helix shows how biochemical phenomena can be related to other phenomena usually studied in many different fields from genetics and cell biology to organic chemistry.

CONCLUSION

The suggestion of this chapter is probably best summarised by an exhortation not to give up in the face of the theoretical mêlée that seems to be going on in sociology. The toings and froings, the arguments and counter-arguments, the assertions and denials, may on first viewing strike one as impossible to follow. But, with a little patience and a willingness to see the different positions that are adopted as outcomes of defensible choices that are made, some sense of what is going on can be arrived at. The choices reflect the interests, attitudes, and predispositions of those who construct theories as well as their views of what theorising ought to be about. It is our hope that once the newcomer to sociology sees this, and sees also that differences of opinion on such matters are probably irresolvable, then, rather than backing off in dismay, he or she will feel free to join in and hence begin to enjoy the sociology 'game'. The thing is, and it is often forgotten, that theories, though solutions to problems in the sense we outlined earlier, are also essential to investigations. In other words, listing, deciding, confirming, deciding the worth of a theory is only part of the 'game' so to speak. Without theories we would not know what to investigate let alone how to do it.

FURTHER READING

R HARRÉ, *The Philosophies of Science*, Oxford University Press, 1972. Provides a summary and discussion of some of the salient views on science and the role of theory.

G HOMANS, *The Nature of Social Science*, Harcourt Brace, 1967. A statement of his theory.

O LEWIS, *La Vida*, Panther, 1968. A brilliant example of a 'realist' style of theorising.

C W MILLS, *The Power Elite*, Oxford University Press, 1956. Presents Mills' analysis of the distribution of power in American society.

T PARSONS, 'The Distribution of Power in American Society', in his *Politics and Social Structure*, Free Press, 1969. Parsons' analysis.

M WEBER, 'Science as Vocation', in H H Gerth and C W Mills (eds), *From Max Weber: Essays in Sociology*, Routledge, 1967. A statement on the 'ethical neutrality' of science.

Chapter 5
MAKING SOCIOLOGY A SCIENCE

Throughout this book, not surprisingly since it is a topic of major concern to sociology, we have raised the matter of sociology's scientific status. In this chapter we will take this up much more thoroughly. In particular, we shall try to show that there is a range of choices on offer for how to make sociology more scientific. One view is that sociology should mirror, or be symmetrical with, science in that its explanations should follow the same logic as those used in the natural sciences. Another is that sociology's explanations should relate to those provided by natural science. In what follows, we shall look at both of these and show that while there are strong arguments in their favour, there are equally strong reservations to express, especially with regard to the limitations and requirements we would need to impose upon sociology whichever of the choices were to be made. We will not discuss those views which argue that a scientific sociology is neither possible nor desirable. Instead, we will focus only on the suggestions made by those who are convinced that sociology is, or could be, scientific. This will allow us to indicate something of the counter-arguments without complicating the discussion unduly. It is our intention to be entirely neutral as to whether sociology should or should not be scientific. We will confine ourselves to examining what would be involved if any of the proposals were to be followed up in a serious and consistent way.

One of the advantages of picturing sociology as a collection of games devoted, among other things, to the play of ideas is that we do not have to prejudge the scientific status of the discipline to determine how we are to engage in it, but can treat the attainment of scientific status as one of the ways in which sociologists might choose to play. This means we can avoid treating it as a metaphysical question, the answer to which crucially determines whether and how we can play at all. Instead we can examine the issue from a different angle entirely and ask, 'Given we want to constitute a scientific sociology, how might we go about it?'. We shall need to remember that there could be more than one way of 'playing' scientific sociology. Fortunately for us, as it happens, three broad strategies can be discerned in this particular debate. The first looks for similarities and differences between socio-logical theories and those of the natural sciences. The second tries to bring out and strengthen interconnections between sociological theories and those of human sciences such as psychology which are obviously more akin to the natural sciences. The third highlights and seeks to improve the objectivity of sociology's methods of research.

At the introductory level, it has been this last which has dominated. Much time in texts and courses is given over to examining ranges of research strategy and just how and why they do or do not preserve 'scientific objectivity'. We feel, though, that this concentration has been somewhat misleading. Decisions concerning the style of research strategy to be followed depend upon prior decisions about the kind of science sociology might hope to be. Before we could say, for instance, that we wanted a research strategy which facilitated the testing of hypotheses, we would, as a precondition, have to accept that sociological predictions amenable to testing could be formulated. We would also have to have some idea of the scope of the hypotheses we were trying to develop as well, perhaps, as some notion of how, as they were accumulated, they might be connected up with hypotheses being developed elsewhere, in psychology, social biology, economics, linguistics, and so on. Decisions about the appropriateness and objec-tivity of methods of research, then, follow on from decisions made about more general matters. For this reason, we shall limit ourselves to these prior decisions. Naturally, we shall allude here and there to the implications which particular lines of choice might have for the style of research that can be carried out. However, in this chapter methods of social research will not be of primary interest.

From the divergence of views to be found in the discipline, it is fairly obvious that, at least for the foreseeable future, there is unlikely to be universal agreement on how to assess or justify sociology's claim to scientific status. There is, so to say, no royal road to science. It is precisely because nothing is settled that those coming to sociology for the first time find the debate over its scientific status so frustrating. No one seems to know just what it would take to resolve matters once and for all. We will try to elucidate what is involved, not by comparing and contrasting the general schemes currently available, but by asking what would be required of sociology were it to adopt one or other of the forms of explanation usually associated with the natural sciences.

We will also look at what is implied if sociology were to seek strong affiliations with some of the more natural science oriented social sciences such as psychology. We take it that any general set of proposals for making sociology scientific would contain recommendations for the types of explanations to be sought, the nature of the relationships to be fostered with contiguous disciplines, as well as suggestions concerning the research strategies which might be adopted.

But to start with, why is it so difficult to decide whether sociology is or is not a science? One reason that is generally offered is the relative youthfulness of the discipline. It is said that it still has to lay its foundations upon which to build up its store of theories and findings. The natural sciences emerged from traditions which bequeathed them whole bodies of accumulated knowledge which could be taken up, organised, and displaced. Sociology developed in the social, political, and philosophical maelstrom of the late eighteenth and early nineteenth centuries. As yet it has not had time to make firm enough progress to lay secure theories and findings to allow a Newton, a Dalton, or a Darwin to emerge. It is not simply, or so this argument implies, that sociologists do not agree upon what is involved in the aspiration to match the natural sciences, but rather that, at the moment, they are in no position to realise any such aspiration.

A second reason that has been offered for sociology's failure to make unambiguous progress as a science is the complexity of its subject-matter. Although the phenomena of the natural sciences often appear to be amazingly complex at first sight, in fact the investigative strategy of science, it is said, is simplification. Complex processes are systematically reduced to simple ones. It seems to many that, out of necessity perhaps, sociology goes about things the other way around. What are, on the face of it, routine, simple, straightforward matters of daily life become under sociological scrutiny complex and highly ramified. Thus sociological accounts of ordinary things such as the games children play, contain complex interweavings of explanations which invoke differential child-rearing practices, the needs of a stable social system, the relationship between role models and social control, primary and secondary socialisation, and much, much more. The difficulty for sociology, it is said, is retaining clarity *and* simplicity.

This is often related to another reason why sociology has not become scientific. Because of the difficulty of retaining simplicity, it is often necessary to allow a number of alternative explanatory mechanisms to operate all at once. In the case of the children's games example, we might find gender and class explanations being set side by side. These are then interconnected by recourse to a more generalised explanation devised to cover all cases. Class and gender are aspects of role learning, say, or are reducible to one another, or whatever. It is, so to speak, only a question of ingenuity in seeing how they are really the same, or really aspects of something else. In contrast, while the demonstration that relativity theory could encompass Newton's laws of mechanics was a matter of ingenuity, it was also much more. It required a great deal of painstaking, preliminary work to be done, discovering under what conditions the classical laws did not hold or did not furnish immediately acceptable explanations. This difference between sociological and natural science theories is recognisable in the apparent mutual exclusivity and self-supporting character of general theories in sociology, and the tendency to treat them as competing paradigms.

As we said at the outset, given the lack of agreement on sociology's claim to scientific status, we are faced with choices to make. Often these choices are presented as complementary. Once decisions are made with regard to the kind of explanations wanted then it will be possible to follow through their logic by making connections with the other social sciences. We will separate these choices, while at the same time, retaining an awareness of their possible implications for each other. This will enable us to concentrate on what we think are the two most important themes to be brought out. First, what is entailed in making one decision rather than another and how might this affect the sort of sociology 'games' that could be played? Second, in making particular choices what are we committing ourselves to? What are the internal requirements and standards imposed by particular choices? Once we have a fair idea of these two, then we should have an appreciation of why the question of sociology's scientific status remains so controversial.

THE SYMMETRY OF EXPLANATION

We will start with the claim that if sociology is to be scientific, there must be a similarity, or symmetry, between the forms of explanation it offers and those of the natural sciences. An explanation we will take to be a story which makes a set of outcomes or events expectable. It does this by linking these outcomes to other events. It is the form of the link which marks the type of explanation. However, before looking at this in detail, there is one thing to note. Even in science, there are different kinds of explanation which work in particular ways. Moreover, explanations work at differing levels of generality. The explanation that a kettle boils because of the heat given out by the electric element it contains might satisfy an inquiring five-year-old, but a much older child might want to know how the element works, how the heat transfer takes place, and so on. To satisfy this child we would have to speak of resistances in circuits and transformations in forms of energy. The first explanation would have to be *explicated* to provide the second. One way of describing this process is to call the first explanation an 'explanation sketch', and the process of explication 'the provision of secondary elaboration'. It is how the connections are made in the secondary elaborations that gives the different forms of explanations their titles. So, we will look in this regard at causal, functional, and genetic explanations, to see how they are used in science and how they might be used in sociology.

There is one other thing to bear in mind. The process of explication has, as a general rule, gone much further in the natural sciences than it has in sociology and, indeed, in most of the other social sciences. We often find that generally accepted explanations in sociology rest upon secondary elaborations that have not themselves been explicated. This can be illustrated by comparing the theory of natural selection as an account of species differentiation with sociological theories of social change. All that the former requires is three elments: (a) that the process of random mutation carry on over (b) an enormous time span with (c) different mutations having different survival values. With just these elements, natural selection explains species differentiation. The theory does not need a prime mover, a grand design, nor an end state towards which evolution is moving. It is difficult to think of a general theory of social change, or any sociological theory for that matter, which has so few elements and which does not require us to grant a whole host of secondary elaborations about the essential nature of history, the psychological make-up of human beings, the relative fixedness of the stages to be passed through, and so on. In other words, compared with many scientific theories, sociological ones seem overburdened with adjustments to make them convincing: an observation, of course, relevant to the complicating character of sociological theories noted earlier.

It is now time to look in some detail at the types of explanation suggested for sociology.

Causal explanations

Probably the most popular suggestion that is made for strengthening sociology's scientific claims is that it should offer causal explanations.

But, what exactly is a causal explanation in science and what would producing one require of sociology? A fairly simple example might be of value here. If yeast and sugar are dissolved in water and the mixture maintained at a temperature of about 70°F, eventually an alcoholic potion will result. It may not be all that pleasant to drink but grape juice or blackberry juice might help. The process of fermentation converts the sugar to alcohol. It is this which causally explains the presence of the alcohol. It is only after the yeast has acted upon the sugar that the alcohol is present. So, a first characteristic to note about standard causal explanations is that there is a temporal sequence of cause and effect. A second characteristic is the fact that the sugar, yeast, and alcohol are all distinct entities, and the mixing of the sugar and yeast is a separate event from the later production of alcohol. The third feature of causal explanations is not so immediately apparent but follows from the other two. Whenever the required conditions are satisfied, the causal process will occur. The 'constant conjunction' of yeast and sugar solution, given the right temperature, will provide us with alcohol.

The first two features of causal explanations have been the subject of much discussion of late, particularly in the light of developments in high-energy physics. The third has always been contentious. It has been argued that it is impossible to specify all the conditions which must be in constant conjunction for some process to occur. The fermentation of sugar requires water, heat, and yeast. It also depends upon our paying the electricity bill, the functioning of the heating system, the purity of the ingredients, and, presumably, the continuation of the universe in the way that it has up until now. Although a little fanciful, this does indicate just why it is said that it is never 'actually' possible to determine whether all the conditions are in place, in which case we can never 'really' ensure constant conjunction, replicate experiments, test predictions, or generalise from one set of findings to another. To defuse this objection, causal explanations make use of a very important device known as the *ceteris paribus* clause; that is, all other things being equal, when sugar and yeast are dissolved in water, fermentation occurs. This *ceteris paribus* clause allows causal explanations to simplify what would otherwise be impossibly complex sets of conditions. It allows for the formulation of a certain research strategy for it demands we indicate the scope of the relevant test conditions. By the isolation and manipulation of conditions, one can come to know just what, *ceteris paribus*, is to be in constant conjunction. The *ceteris paribus* clause, in other words, underpins the rationale of the logico-experimental method.

Thus far our description of fermentation is no more than an explanation sketch. A great deal more would be needed for it to be an acceptable causal explanation in science. A biochemist might begin to fill out the explanation by rewriting the description as follows:

$$C_6h_{12}O_6 \longrightarrow 2CO_2 + 2C_2H_5OH + energy$$

Using chemical symbols this says that glucose in the presence of an enzyme is transformed into carbon dioxide, ethanol, and energy. What is important about this new description is not that it uses scientific symbols, nor that it embodies mathematical notation, but that it indicates just where the *causal mechanism* producing the transformation is to be found. It is the anaerobic respiration of the yeast which breaks down the glucose. Our biochemist, of course, might be interested in pursuing things much further. How exactly does the enzyme work? Why is water necessary since it is unused? How is the energy released? But, no matter how much further the explanation is taken, it still remains true that the explanation of the presence of the alcohol is the fermentation of sugar by the yeast.

The process of secondary elaboration is a process of rewriting which could be expressed in this diagram:

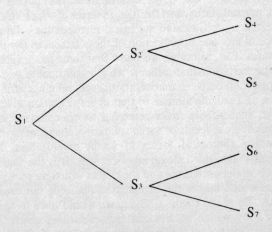

Sentences about glucose, yest, and sugar

Sentences about primary sugars, catalysts, and respiration in enzymes

Sentences about chemical bonding, biochemiical processes, proteins, and forms of energy

The central element in causal explanations, then, is the specification of a causal mechanism which makes the connection between the initial conditions and the effects which they cause. Without a causal mechanism there can be no causal explanation. It is at this crucial point that the difficulties for sociology can be brought into view. Although great efforts have been made to quantify variables and mathematise relationships, sociology has had considerable trouble in identifying clear and precise causal mechanisms akin to those of the biochemist. Consequently, its causal explanations are relatively weak ones. For a number of very good reasons, sociologists are unable to exercise the degree of strict control over the conditions to which the *ceteris paribus* clause is applied. The consequence is that while the biochemist can simplify conditions in rewriting explanations, the sociologist has very little idea what might be central conditions and which the marginal ones for the processes under scrutiny. The consequent fear of distortion leads to the inclusion of unexplicated variables in the secondary elaborations which connect the intitial conditions and the effects or outcomes.

A classic example, that of suicide, will serve as a good indication of what we are talking about here. As a result of numerous studies, sociologists are fairly confident that they have identified a series of factors such as age, sex, religious affiliation, occupation, place of residence, marital status, and the like, in terms of which suicide rates vary. There are sophisticated statistical methods for estimating the importance of any one or collection of these factors in the variations between rates. But, although we know that some factors account for more of the variation than others, we are still unable to provide a causal connection between marital status, age, religious affiliation, or occupation and suicide similar to that of fermentation given by the biochemist. Instead, we make reference to unexplicated secondary elaborations such as levels of social solidarity, suicidogenic currents, normal and pathological forms of social organisation, levels of anomie, and vulnerable categories of persons. It is the vagueness of the connection between these and the effects which they are supposed to produce which makes the explanation plausible but causally unconvincing. To make them stronger, we would have to specify the mechanisms by which such social factors as age, gender, marital status, and religion could, through the intervention of variables like the pathological forms of social solidarity, produce particular levels of suicide. By themselves, quantification and the analogous use of the logico-experimental method are not sufficient.

Failure to appreciate the role which causal mechanisms play in causal explanations can lead to two misapprehensions. The first is the belief that the difficulties we have just been discussing have been obviated by the use of what are sometimes known as 'causal models'. By means of various techniques using inferential statistics, such models evaluate the contribution which selected variables make to the overall variance of some phenomenon. Because, say, marital status or age categories might be correlated with variations in the rates of suicide or mental illness, they are said to explain or cause more of the variance. However, because these statistical models are not the direct equivalent of the scientist's experiment or the engineer's mock-up, this use of cause is likely to remain vague unless we can specify just how factors like these are causally connected to suicide or mental illness. No matter how sophisticated the model, unless these connections are explicated, it does not really causally explain anything. All it does is tell us that *somehow* variations in age and marital status increase the probability that one is prone to suicide, mental illness, or whatever. The key sociological question of how they might do so remains unanswered.

The second misapprehension is that symmetry with the natural sciences might still be preserved even if we have to use the notion of cause in a less strict, more general way than we have been discussing so far. We could do this, it might be thought, by offering causal explanations similar to those on offer in history. With this weaker form of causal explanation neither constant conjunction nor the provision of a causal mechanism is required. When historians speak of causes, what they are pointing to are the reasons for some particular occurrence, what brought it about, not a cause in the natural science sense of the term. If a historian were to suggest that hyperinflation followed by economic collapse was one of the causes of the rise of Nazism in post-Weimar Germany, or that the influx of bullion from the Americas was one of the causes of the development of capitalism, all that would be being said is that without those factors the subsequent pattern of events would have been different. What is certainly not being said is that there is a readily identifiable causal mechanism to hand to make the connection between economic conditions and political ideologies, or that hyperinflation coupled with recession always gives rise to Nazi-type political movements. Looking back on those particular historical circumstances as they turned out, we can say that this or that factor appears to have made the difference. Even though this might be important and valuable to know, it is not causal in the natural science sense.

There are several lessons to be learned from the discussion so far.

First and foremost, it ought to be quite clear by now that causal explanations are particular kinds of explanation and very difficult to arrive at. They require not only patience, the accumulation of findings, and attention to detail, but may only fit certain kinds of phenomena, for example those archetypally dealt with by some of the natural sciences. To try to offer causal explanations for phenomena other than these may mean having to use cause in a much weaker sense. It might well imply, too, that in this weaker form such causal explanations will have to be explicated by making use of concepts such as interpretation, meaning, rationality, and motivation which have been notoriously difficult to treat in the natural science sense of cause and yet which do constitute an abiding interest for sociology. Of course, if psychology were to be able to establish a causal connection between mental events such as those mentioned and social behaviour, it could be argued that all might be easier. We will look at this later on. In any event, one important cost of incorporating causal thinking into sociology in the strictest terms, might be a narrowing of the range of phenomena that could be investigated and the interest to be taken in them. The net effect of this delimiting side constraint of causal connectiveness, if applied across the board, could be to change the fundamental shape and scope of sociology, which may or may not be a good thing. However, if sociology were to aspire to the causal form, that is to want to play the 'game' of offering causal explanations, then the specification of sociologically adequate causal mechanisms is a priority and not the accumulation of quantified variables. More than this, such causal mechanisms ought, in principle, to have a rewrite potentiality as well, one which would enable the connection between, say, sociology and psychology to be made clearly and precisely.

Fulfilling this assignment would be a very tough business indeed. In fact, we would be hard put to it to think of any one social science which has been able to provide the kind of connection which we are saying is essential to the causal form of explanation, not even economics. A great deal has been heard recently of the control of the demand for money as an efficient cure for inflation. If the price of money (interest rate) is raised, the demand for money will fall and hence, eventually, so will inflation. The explanation which is offered for this connects up the total demand for money, the liquidity preferences of firms and individuals, general levels of prices, levels of employment, and so on. But these connections are *rationalisations*, even though they may be amenable to, or even derived from, mathematical and graphical expressions. They do not constitute the setting out of causal mechanisms. The argument works only if, *ceteris paribus*, we are prepared to treat firms as individuals and other individuals as ourselves. We have to generalise our 'rationality' to other economic actors to provide the thread of plausibility which the monetarist story has. If the price of borrowing rose, we would reduce our borrowing and firms would do the same by cutting costs, holding wages steady, and by becoming more efficient. Such a picture may be a perfectly reasonable one, but it is not *de facto* a causal one. This can be attested to by the simple observation that when rates of interest were first raised, firms borrowed even more because *in the short run* they could not afford not to. The connection between rates of interest and falling inflation is a chain of rationalisations not of causal connections, despite its formulation in quantified terms. In order to provide a causal chain of connections, economists would have to reduce the scope of their *ceteris paribus* assumption about basic economically rational actors and hence introduce many other, potentially disruptive, non-rationalisable side constraints such as the personality of ministers and financiers, luck, and serendipity.

The constant conjunction characteristic of causal explanations has led to them being dubbed 'predictivist'. Certainly many of the causal explanations of natural science do have this character. What this means is that they have a built-in logic for evaluation, namely the testing of predictions. This is why causalism, predictivism, and the logico-experimental method are so closely entwined. Sociology, as we have seen, is almost wholly bereft of candidates for causal explanation. It is often said that this is why sociology can only produce weak generalisations of the statistical sort. These take the form of probability or trend statements. When, sometime in the future, sociology is able to put causal explanations together which provide tight causal connnections between conditions and their effects, then universal, predictive generalisations will be available. On this view, the generation of statistical hypotheses and generalisations is a symptom of sociology's scientific immaturity. The trouble with this hope is that quantum mechanics, a branch of one of the most mature of the sciences, physics, only produces statistical generalisations, although these are the product of very sophisticated causal mechanisms. The causal account provides for the statistical nature of the regularities. Statistical generalisations, then, are not themselves characteristic of an immaturity in science, and cannot be justified solely by weak causality. It would seem to follow that, *if* sociology aspires to causalist explanations while at the same time maintaining that it can only have statistical regularities, *then* it will be necessary for it to develop some explanatory account similar to Heisenberg's Uncertainty Principle to demonstrate, as a real explanatory device and not as a methodological apology, why this state of affairs *has* to be so.

What have we got so far? It seems that the central characteristic of causal explanations is the provision of causally efficient connections between conditions and their effects. The power of many natural science explanations resides in their facility for explication into many elaborately rewritten but none the less precisely connected versions of one another. This is no mean achievement, and in all cases is the product of many investigators spending untold hours accumulating a base for such explication. Sociology seems to lack the base of findings that science has. If it is to aspire to accommodation within, or symmetry with, the natural sciences on the grounds considered so far, it is this stiff test which it will have to pass. It will have to show just how the explanation sketches which it offers could be filled out. At the same time, unless it is going to argue that the statistical generalisations which it offers are simply the effect of it being arrested at an adolescent stage, an argument which it is hard to credit, then the unpredictability of outcomes has to be built in as a causal matter. To do all of this will require sociology to engage upon a programme of painstakingly slow accumulation of findings relevant to and amenable to treatment in causalist terms. This will inevitably mean a piecemeal approach to generalisation and, perhaps more significant, maybe a change in the nature of the phenomena brought under sociological scrutiny.

Functional explanations

Because of the difficulties inherent in the adoption of causal explanations, it is sometimes suggested that sociology might become scientific by using functional explanations similar to those found in biology. And, of course, there are links of a more general kind between sociology and biology. First, as embodied beings our social lives are bound to be intimately interrelated with our biological lives. This is a theme to which we will return. Second, there are strong historical links between the disciplines through anthropology and the influence that organicist ideas such as those of Spencer and the Social Darwinians have had both in sociology and in anthropology. Accordingly, it is plausible to argue that rather than physics or chemistry, it is biology which sociology should try to emulate. Indeed, sociology may very well have achieved symmetry with biology, for well-known and well-established functional explanations abound in sociology.

In a functional explanation a phenomenon is explained by reference to the role which it plays within an environment of conditions. The explanation consists in specifying the phenomenon's contribution to the preservation of the conditions. If a biologist wishes to explain why mice have whiskers, why zebras are striped, why pine trees have needle-like leaves, why bears are relatively rare and earthworms numerous, or why baleen whales have a peculiarly shaped palate, reference will be made to the role that whiskers, stripes, palates, and so on play for the species concerned, or its place in the food chain. Such explanations involve the identification of a generalised and strategically important need that the item in question can satisfy for the species as a whole. Functional explanations do not aim to account for why *this* mouse has whiskers, *this* zebra stripes, or *this* whale an odd palate. Each item is taken as an instance of the class as a whole.

Functional explanations, then, utilise a broad-ranging strategy. This consists in the supposition that primary needs, food, shelter, and reproduction in biology's case, will be met in differing ways within different environments. The peculiarity of local conditions will shape the adaptations required to satisfy the needs. Hence, mice have whiskers because these are efficient sensing devices in narrow dark spaces. Zebra have black stripes because this marking effectively breaks up the animals outline given that its major predators see monochromatically. The connection between needs for survival and the item to be explained is made by pointing to the efficiency of the item within the given environment of conditions and by secondary elaborations which, in biology's case, make use of such concepts as survival value, ecological niche, and natural selection.

Exactly the same form of explanation can be observed in the two most prominent theoretical clusters in sociology, namely Marxism and Functionalism. Both point to the net contribution which some phenomenon makes to the preservation of existing social relationships. They do this by positing certain needs necessary for society's continued existence. For example, Marxism and Functionalism agree that there are clear differences in levels of political power in our society. They also agree that it is a fact of social life that these differences are associated with other differences such as those of wealth and status. The rich and the prestigious tend to be the more powerful. Both theories explain the existence of such differences by indicating their contribution to the continuation of existing social relationships. It is at this point that they part company. Functionalism suggests that in every society there will be some roles which are thought, by the members of society, to be more important than others. These roles will vary from society to society. It is then argued that each society then arranges its affairs so as to ensure that these important roles are filled. This is done by making these roles more attractive than others by attaching wealth, power, and status to them. Hence individuals are encouraged to compete for them and the most talented, as the society in question defines that term, will perform the roles. Thus the distinctions between the wealthy and the poor, the powerful and the powerless, those of high and low status function to distribute the available talent as effectively as possible.

The Marxist explanatory strategy is much the same. This time what is at stake is the continuation of a basic inequality in the means of production of material life. Inequalities of power and status arise because of the need to preserve this basic inequality. This is achieved through the domination of one group over others; the domination of the owners of the means of production over the rest. In order to retain its domination, the dominant class reserves political power and high social status to itself. The high prestige which the wealthy and powerful have helps to mask the strains inherent in the continuation of the basic inequality. Without it, the existing pattern of relations would be threatened and unstable. Both Marxism and Functionalism, then, see the institutionalisation of power and status differentiation as a strategy for ensuring the survival of existing social relationships. Where they differ is how these arrangements are to be described.

The first thing to notice about functional explanations is that they are explanations only in a special sense. They consist of conglomerations of related concepts all of which are connected by means of a *picture* of existing conditions. Far from being explanations in a causal sense, what is offered is a functional description utilising a particular package of theoretically defined concepts. Using the idea which we introduced earlier, we could call these descriptions *rationalisations* of the items under investigation. To say of a distribution of power, for instance, that it works in the way that it does because of the contribution which it makes to the preservation of a form of social life is, in fact, to attribute a rationale to it. Activities such as the making of particular policy decisions by office-holders can then be rationalised, that is described, in terms of the contribution which these decisions make to the continuation of the existing state of affairs. For a functional explanation, the crucial element is not the connection between the condition and its consequence, as it was with causalism, but the *plausibility* of the rationale that is invoked. Functional explanations only succeed if we are convinced by the rationale. This is just as true for biology as it is for sociology. The explanation of why hoverflies look like wasps, why polar bears are white, and why humans have opposable thumbs is that all of these are locally efficient methods of fulfilling fixed biological needs. Once we accept this story, so to speak, we can go on to fill the explanation out using notions such as random mutation, competition for space and food, species differentiation, and so on. If we did not accept the story that such differences emerged over a long period of time because they were so efficient, and sought to explain their existence in some other way, then all the secondary elaboration would fall.

In sociology the rationale of functional explanations is that of need fulfilment. Marxism tells this story by seeing social life as historically determined; Functionalism sees social life as rationally constructed. This is a very good example of what, earlier in this book, we called the exercising of options. We are free to choose between these two on the basis of the relative attraction we feel for the internal features of the explanations that are offered, the fact that they deal with topics we are interested in, for example, or because they set up problems in stimulating ways. The plausibility of the rationale is grounded in concerns such as these.

The use of functional explanations does allow us, then, to draw some fairly close parallels between sociology and one of the natural sciences. It does so without the prohibitive side constraints consequent upon causalism. Unfortunately, this is not all. For biologists, functional explanations are heuristic in character; that is, first approximations circumscribing the locale within which causal explanations will have to be sought. The fit between some characteristic and the environmental conditions could, in principle, be explicated using causal explanations compiled from biochemistry and elsewhere. The causal explanation would then provide the infrastructure on which the functional explanation stands. It does not matter that as yet biology may be unable to provide this infrastructure in all cases. In principle, it ought to be possible to do it. To take just one example, the explanation of the stripes of zebra might be rewritten in terms associated with causal accounts of perception and the consequences that different markings might have on predation, variation in the gene pool, and the role of DNA in inheritance. This is not to say that functional explanations in biology are inadequate, far from it. But it is to say that a particular explanatory strategy may be involved in their use. This might be extremely troublesome if it were to be extended to sociology, for it would land us back with all the difficulties of causal explanation discussed in the previous section. If we want to say that the relationship between functional and causal theories need not hold for sociology, then it becomes that much more difficult to claim a close symmetry between sociology and biology.

A second feature which militates against the close parallel between sociology and biology is the permanent choice of rationales sociology offers. In biology only one, that of Darwinianism, has come to dominate. Competing theories were set aside. This is not an argument against the use of functional explanations in sociology, but it ought to warn us against expecting that because it has adopted such explanations, sociology will make the same progress that biology has. Developments in biology could well have been so rapid because investigations concentrated on one rationale.

Functional explanations are attractive because they do not lay down the stringent requirements that causal ones do. We might feel then that if one bona fide science can use them widely, so too can sociology. One major problem, though, is the fact that the rationales of functional explanations appear to be self-supporting. In biology this has been obviated by treating functional explanations as first approximations and by concentrating on one rationale only. In sociology, however, functional explanations do not appear to be a first step towards, nor a species of, causal explanation, and the choice of rationales is open. As a consequence, the hoped for symmetry between sociology and this particular natural science looks doubtful. If it is symmetry we are after, we may well have to seek it elsewhere.

Genetic explanations

Many sciences such as zoology, geophysics, and botany make use of genetic explanations. Broadly, a genetic explanation offers the story behind or the 'natural history' of an event or course of events. Geophysics provides a readily understandable instance of what is meant here. Using the theory of plate tectonics, geophysicists are able to explain the occurrence of earthquakes, volcanoes, and other seismic activity by relating them to the phases that zones on the margins of plates pass through. The earthquakes and volcanoes associated with the western seaboard of the North American continent, for example, are explained by the collision of a plate under the Pacific ocean with one containing the landmass of Canada and the USA. The present level, frequency, and type of seismic activity are characteristic of the early stages in which one plate overrides another. As this process continues, the zone of contact will shift and what is at present a very active area will pass into more quiescent phases. Similar developmental explanations are to be found in astrophysics, accounting, for example, for the origins, growth, and decay of stellar masses, and in botany for the development of climax states of vegetation types.

Genetic explanations are also extremely popular in sociology. They range from accounts of particular phenomena or processes, the professionalisation of welfare provision in Western Europe, for example, or the history of particular pieces of industrial unrest, to general processes such as urbanisation, industrialisation, and the development of the state. It is important to remember that a genetic explanation is not a causal one simply because historical succession does not necessarily imply a causal connection. Even where the weaker sense of causation might be applied, as we outlined earlier, a genetic explanation does not pick out for emphasis those conditions which make significant differences. It is here that the uses of genetic explanations in sociology and science tend to differ. Just as with functional explanation, genetic explanations in the natural sciences have the character of first approximations. They provide a brief sketch of the range of things involved which ought, in principle at any rate, to be rewritable in strict causal terms. It ought to be possible to unpack the genetic explanation encompassed in plate tectonics into causal explanations given by physics. Certainly the sorts of causal mechanisms which would be needed are well enough known. In sociology, yet again, this does not appear to be the case. As with functional explanations, genetic explanations are viewed as alternatives to causal accounts, not proxies for them.

One of the more attractive features of genetic explanations is that they do not have to be general in form. They can be constructed to apply to only a very narrow range of particular instances. As we saw in Chapter 4, Weber's account of the rise of capitalism and its relation to the Puritan theodicy might be better understood if it were regarded as a very specific genetic explanation and not a putative, generalising, causal one. So might Lofland's social psychological theory of the reasons why individuals join religious cults, or Erving Goffman's account of the institutionalisation of mental patients. In all of these cases, the strength of the explanation is found in its narrative form. Either we are carried along and persuaded by it, or we are not. But while this is a strength, it is also, for many, a major difficulty in the path of claiming an unarguable scientific status for the use of such explanations in sociology. Because there is no in-principle resort to causal explanations to fill out the genetic account as there appears to be in the natural sciences, there are no obvious ways of objectively determining the status of competing explanations. There can be no reference to 'the facts of the matter', so to speak, because the genetic explanation, like the functional one, selects and organises for itself what are to count as the facts. We are left to make judgements based on criteria internal to the explanation such as its stimulation for further research, its novelty, the fit between it and other explanations, and so on. It is this lack of certainty which disturbs many commentators.

None of the three major forms of explanation which we have surveyed looks as if it is going to provide sociology with an easy route to unambiguous scientific status. Functional and genetic explanations seem able to provide only a partial symmetry, which is not to say, of course, that they are inadequate or have no role to play. The strongest case for scientific explanation in sociology would consist in the formulation of clear, causal explanations. Unfortunately this may be extremely difficult to do and may have overly restrictive consequences. It might mean, for instance, that sociology would have to adopt a version of the logico-experimental method and redefine its phenomena in strict causal terms. There are many ethical and practical reasons why the former may be unattractive, while the latter might mean a wholly new conceptual structure would have to be developed for the discipline. Notions of choice, motivation, action based on interpretation, and so forth would have to be fundamentally reconsidered.

REDUCTION TO SCIENCE

However, there is another way that we could set about making sociology more clearly scientific, that is by reducing to or complementing sociological explanations, be they causal, functional, or genetic, by natural science ones. This might take one of two forms. We could take up the suggestion that sociology is 'really' reducible to some bona fide natural science. The favourite for this is biology. The second form is to say that sociology's explanations require filling out by those drawn from other disciplines, and here the most popular choice is psychology. As we said earlier, for many psychology is but one remove from biology, neurophysiology, and, hence, the rest of the natural sciences. In the rest of this chapter, we will look at both of these suggestions and the implications that adopting either one of them might have.

Sociology and biology

In its clearest form the proposal we will look at says that sociological phenomena are, in fact, wholly explicable in biological terms. Sociology could become scientific by transforming itself into socio-biology. The arguments here are, briefly, as follows. Using concepts drawn from population dynamics, of late biology has been relatively successful in explaining various forms of animal behaviour. Behaviour traits which increase the likelihood of a species' survival will be preserved. Those which are disadvantageous are eradicated. Such traits may well be social in character, mating displays or alarm signalling, or they may be purely physical, as with the form of locomation or type of vision. When seeking to explain the existence of any particular trait, the biologist looks for the relative advantage which it might offer. This holds for behavioural traits too, such as the dominance hierarchy among chimpanzees, the communal farming of leaf-cutting ants, or the division of labour among honey bees. All these are said to contribute to the continuation of the species because they have survival value. To fill out the explanation, it is necessary to show how the hierarchy reduces wasteful competition for females, the division of labour increases efficiency, and so on. Since, for the biologist, there are only minor differences between man as a species and our nearest primate relatives, and since there is also a continuity of explanation throughout the animal kingdom, that which explains animal behaviour can be used to explain human behaviour. Human kinship systems, the human division of labour, forms of economic development, even philosophising, can all be viewed as behavioural traits which exist because they have survival value. Particular traits such as arranged marriages, the factory system, and Western rationalism can be explained as local adaptations to circumstances. Their survival value is then explicated through the secondary elaboration of concepts drawn from population dynamics, the regulation of food resources, control of population, the need for organisation.

There is a great deal that can be gained by looking at human social life in this way. It imbues it with the same fascination that we often find in biologists' accounts of termites, chimpanzees, ants, and so on. But whatever the advantage, the net result is to reduce sociology to biology by reducing sociological phenomena to biological ones. In the scheme as we have outlined it, there is very little room for a distinctively sociological interest to flourish. Sociologists are not much interested in why particular behavioural traits persist but are much more concerned to see how patterns of behaviour emerge and intermesh. Their interest is in how social relationships are organised and reproduced, and the notion of survival value is unlikely to be of much help with this.

This difference of interest can be brought out in a number of ways. To begin with, although for the biologist the differences between ourselves and the apes may be minimal, for the sociologist, as facts of social life, such differences are overwhelming. We do not treat apes in the way that we treat other people. We maintain an important distinction between human life and animal; a distinction which has all kinds of consequences of interest to the sociologist. It does not matter that there may be many philosophical and moral objections to having a distinction of the kind that we do have, none the less it is there and it is used by most people. It is expressed in the expectations which we have of other people but not of animals, the responsibility which we attribute to them for their actions, and the treatment which we think they merit. Despite our tendency to anthropomorphise animals, often for purely manipulative reasons or to make important ethical points, for example about vivisection, the line between animal and human life is still there. Indeed, much of the reductionism of socio-biology may well be based upon anthropomorphism. It is difficult to imagine what a continuity between our lives and those of animals might be like without giving them a quasi-human status. To talk about what it is like to be a bat, a bee, or a chimp, we have to talk about them in our terms. Because we have marriage systems, a division of labour, castes, and military hierarchies, we feel free to talk of swan monogamy, termite slavery, and soldier ants. We even talk about hibernating animals laying in stores. But none of that ought to suggest to us that animals plan and stock up as we do, for to do that they would have to have a version of our culture. There is only any point in blurring the differences between animals and humans, even if these are sometimes difficult to pin down, if all the crucial sociological differences are not going to be allowed any biological signficance.

Here, once again, we come face to face with differences of interests and constraints. The most obvious thing about socio-biology is that it is socio-*biology*. It tends to take little interest in sociological puzzles and problems, and nor should we expect it to. At its most general, sociological interest is bound up with the fact that human activity is meaningful social action and not simply the consequence, either directly or indirectly, of stimuli in the environment. Sociologists want to view social life in this way because that is how we normally picture it ourselves. We assume that people have reasons for what they do, that they plan to achieve goals, and that their actions somehow reflect their desires and motives. This fundamental feature of sociological interest would be ruled out if sociology were to be reduced to biology. There is value in alerting ourselves to the similarities and differences between ourselves and the animals only if, as sociologists, we are going to draw some conclusions from them. It may be that the crucial difference boils down to the fact that we have an elaborated cultural life and they do not. But it is exactly that which is of sociological concern.

Sociology and psychology

The final proposal we will discuss is that sociology might become scientific if it constructed its explanations to fit in with those of psychology. This might be done by reducing all sociological explanations to psychological ones, a line of action which would have much the same order of consequences as we have just discussed with regard to biology. Or, we could assert the autonomy of psychology and sociology but insist that they are so closely related that their explanations should match one another's. This is the suggestion we will consider.

In essence, this autonomous-but-related view rests upon a factor approach to explanation. It assumes that what is needed to give a full account is a list of the psychological and sociological factors involved as well as a weighting of their relative contributions. This approach has been used with regard to a number of social processes, deviance, socialisation, political activism, and perhaps most notoriously, academic achievement. All of these share a similar kind of explanatory strategy which may be best illustrated by taking the most famous case, academic achievement.

None of the social sciences would dispute that some groups of people do less well than others in school, at least in so far as success is measured by academic achievement. Most particularly, members of some racial categories do markedly less well than others. The typical sociological explanation for this lack of success is to relate this 'underachievement' to a variety of disadvantages associated with the racial categories concerned. Members of a particular racial group may share a culture which is at odds with that of the school, may be economically underprivileged and so have a lack of interest in academic work, poor housing, need to leave school early, and so on. Teachers may not expect students from these groups to succeed and so fail to encourage and help them, thereby producing a self-fulfilling prophecy. The key issue in the debate is whether these sociological factors are well enough established to be able to explain all of the variance between groups. Or are there other factors which explain either partially or totally the degree of difference? In general, it is assumed that in addition to the sociological factors, it is necessary to give some weight to psychological variables such as willingness to learn, the need for achievement, personality, and, admittedly the centre of much dispute, inherited IQ. We can now see why it is that these topics are of primary interest to those wishing to defend the autonomy-but-close-relatedness of sociology and psychology. It is obvious, or so it seems to them, that all that is needed is an explanation that combines and weights the various factors. However, the question for us is not whether it is obvious but how it might be done and what its consequences would be. It is not that one cannot proceed in this factorising way, but the suspicion is that if one were to do so then the range and types of interest one could have in topics such as academic achievement, deviance, or whatever would be severely limited. This is because no matter how we arrange the complementarity or combination, in some sense sociological explanations will always be constrained by psychological ones, and vice versa of course. This is because social life is being viewed as the *joint* outcome of sociological and psychological factors. Accordingly one, if not *the*, crucial test of a sociological interest or theory in this area would have to be the contribution which it made to furthering the fit between sociological and psychological explanations. Hence, we would always end up doing our sociology with half an eye on psychology.

As we say, there is nothing inherently wrong in proceeding in this way. Numerous studies and investigations have done so quite successfully. It does have one major disadvanatage which we might feel outweighs the advantages to be gained by adopting the factorising approach. In order to make a fit between psychological and sociological explanations, we will need a common explanatory strategy. And, given the nature of psychology, its commitment to the logico-experimental method, the formulation of general laws, and so forth, it is likely that we would choose causalism. This would match quite neatly the identification of factors. They would become causes in some loose or strict sense. The problem is that sociology would immediately be saddled with all of the difficulties we discussed earlier, but this time they would be even more acute because the causal mechanisms in sociology would have to fit in with the causal mechanisms identified by psychology. It could well be that, unless we were very careful, sociological interests would become subservient to psychological ones. Complementarity would degenerate into domination.

But, if we want to take a sociological interest in something like academic achievement, is this the price we will have to pay? Is there nothing else we can do? We think that there is. The factor approach could be replaced by a standard organisational one which would display a distinctively sociological attitude towards academic achievement without involving us in demarcation disputes with psychology. Such an account might well be cast in classical Functionalist ways and tell us something about the organisation of our society from the fact that IQ, academic achievement, and academic success are so interrelated. It might point to the way that academic success helps to distribute people into roles. It could also identify the themes that are used to defend and legitimise the examination and evaluation systems by linking a graduated examination system to the professionalisation of education and the dissemination of bureaucratic rationality, together with the extension of the academic division of labour and the consequent specialisation of knowledge. The question need not be taken to be the relative importance of IQ and other psychological factors as against environmental and sociological ones with regard to the real causes of academic success or failure, but how the system works in reproducing, justifying, and legitimating itself, and what that tells us about the nature of our society. Whether we choose to adopt this line or not, it is plain that such an organisational explanation does not depend for its adequacy on the reconciliation of psychology and sociology.

But we are still left with the question with which we started. Would we have, thereby, made sociology more scientific? The answer must remain ambivalent. On some counts it might be; on others it would not. But then the achievement of reconciliation might mean that we would have a sociology no one was interested in. In the end, it comes to the interests we have, and the choices we wish to make.

CONCLUSION

It is our view that the achievement of scientific status for sociology is likely to be a difficult business. What we have tried to do in this chapter is examine some of the options involved in striving to attain this goal. Certainly, it is not a status to be had for the asking, as the history of the natural sciences testifies. However, difficult though it might be, we do not say that sociology will never be able to match the achievements of the natural sciences; that is for the future to say. Nevertheless, this conclusion does not imply that sociology is not worth doing. Being scientific is not the intellectual measure of all things. Nor does failure to achieve scientific status mean that an intellectual activity is less than rigorous, less than productive of knowledge, should be taken less than seriously. Quite the contrary, science is but one way of obtaining knowledge of the world, one kind of 'game' we can invent to go about the business of finding out about the world. There are many others whose value it is unnecessary to weigh by scientific criteria. Whether or not sociology is one of these is, as we have pointed out, still a contentious issue. In other words, at the present moment we are in a position to be able to play different 'games' within sociology, some strictly scientific and some not, just to see where they might lead.

FURTHER READING

H BLALOCK, *Causal Models in Social Science*, Macmillan, 1971. The standard work on causalism and social science.

N BLOCK and G DWORKIN, *The I.Q. Argument*, Pantheon Books, 1976. A discussion of the argument related to I.Q.

S J GOULD, *Ever Since Darwin*, Burnett, 1978. A general introduction to how functional theories work in biology.

R HARRÉ, *The Philosphy of Science*, Oxford University Press, 1972. Probably the most relaxed and accessible of general introductions to the philosophy of science and related questions.

A RYAN, *The Philosophy of the Social Sciences*, Macmillan, 1970. Another good general introduction.

S TOULMIN, *Foresight and Prediction*, Hutchinson, 1961. Still general but slightly more technical.

E O WILSON, *Sociobiology*, Belknap, 1975, and *Human Nature*, Harvard University Press, 1978. These provide a wealth of explanation and case studies in the area of sociobiology.

Chapter 6

APPROACHING QUESTIONS OF METHOD

Up to now we have been talking mainly about theorising, and a major aspect of this element of sociology 'games' has to do with relating the theory to the world: a matter which, as we have pointed out on various occasions, is neither easy nor straightforward. However, essential as it is to sociology 'games', the discipline tends to look at this matter as if it involved two distinct activities: a divorce most obviously demonstrated in the ubiquitous distinction between theory courses and methods courses. Although there may be good pragmatic reasons for such a division, both fields are complicated enough; it tends to reinforce the practice of theorising with too little regard for methods and research implications and, the converse, carrying on research as if theorising were someone else's problem.

What we intend to do in this chapter is discuss some general issues raised in the discipline concerning how and by what means sociology is to acquire knowledge of its phenomena. We shall not discuss any of the methods of research currently available to sociology in any detail, but will stick firmly to broader questions which have shaped the way in which the discipline thinks about methods, the role of empirical research, and its connections with theory, and, particularly, with perspectives and approaches. Some of the issues have been touched on before, though here we direct the discussion towards how they have shaped sociology's thinking about methods of research.

When we suggested earlier that sociology is more like philosophy than physics, we were making a relative contrast. The great weight of sociology's concern is not placed, as it is with physics, on empirical matters. However, this does not mean that empirical questions are, as with philosophy, of almost complete insignificance. It is very important to sociology's idea of itself that it is an empirical discipline and much of the philosophical and theoretical discussion that goes on is about how the discipline might best set about doing this. Questions about research method, consequently, occupy a specially important place in sociology because asking how sociology might develop itself as an empirical enterprise seems to be the same as asking what methods it should use.

'Methods struggles' have taken place among social scientists for a long time and they continue today. As far as sociology is concerned, the dispute which has most decisively affected methodological thinking in the discipline has been the argument over 'Positivism'. Although it is an argument about more than methodology, the demarcation between Positivist and anti-Positivist positions is frequently made in terms of kinds of method, broadly whether they exemplify 'quantitative' or 'qualitative' research strategies. These are the very broadest methodological options available to social science: we either employ a research procedure which involves, or even consists in, the use of numbers and other mathematical symbols or we employ a procedure in which these scarcely appear. The division draws a distinction between methods of sociological research such as the survey and the experiment which stand as exemplars of quantitative work, on the one hand, and field-work inquiries using, for example, participant observation, on the other. Although the choice here might seem to be one which ought to be decided on pragmatic grounds of which is best for the research involved it is treated as one imbued with matters of basic principle. The question of method is often seen as fundamental, as coming before and dictating the shape of other commitments that might be made.

The importance that methodological questions still have, and the specific character they take, are in no small part due to the influence of Positivism on sociological thought. It is a tradition which is well grounded in sociology and goes back at least as far as the work of Comte who, if he is not actually the founder of sociology as he is sometimes alleged to be, did coin the discipline's name. Positivism has continued to be influential and there have been times, the immediate post-war period for one example, when it seemed that it would become entrenched as the methodological orthodoxy. Certainly, it was strongly enough entrenched to provoke an energetic reaction, originating from many otherwise different points of view, against its apparent position as the arbiter of correct sociological practice.

Throughout we have tried to argue against the reduction of issues to the simple terms of an opposition between heroes and villains, and in the controversy over Positivism it is supremely important to avoid this. It is particularly important to avoid regarding Positivism as the public enemy number one, especially since the weight of the discussion will be given over to identifying some of the crucial arguments against it. However, at the same time, we should remember that it was not a pacific Positivism which was subjected to a gratuitous assault, that it was not the helpless victim of uncalled for criticism. On the contrary, as we shall see, the attack on Positivism should properly be referred to as 'the counter-attack on Positivism'.

THE COUNTER-ATTACK ON POSITIVISM

What was the dispute over Positivism which gained new life in the early 1960s all about? Those who have some sympathy for Positivism can rightly claim that its point of view was often travestied by its critics and that under its heading many quite different viewpoints were indiscriminately collated. The account we give here is deliberately simplified, reducing the issues to the barest terms for the purpose of introductory argument. So, in these terms the dispute was about two major issues: first, the use of quantitative methods and, second, the use of an hypothesis-testing strategy in social research.

If Positivism had suggested that sociology could be improved by adopting quantitative methods and that its progress be enhanced by sharpening its hypotheses so that they were realistically testable, then there would seem little reason for such intense controversy. However, Positivism did not advance these in such a hesitant and modest spirit. Both recommendations were advanced as the only acceptable, even the only possible, way in which sociology can and should go about its business. It failed to acknowledge any alternatives to its own way and treated sociological work which failed to conform to its standards as wholly illegitimate and time wasting.

This kind of attitude, of course, accompanies the Positivist programme when put forward in its strongest form and is provocative because it is so dismissive of work inspired by other methodologies. They are being told that their work is valueless. Even in its more dilute and moderate forms, Positivism is offensive for its bland assumption that though qualitative methods have some legitimacy this is limited and secondary to proper quantitative work. This is an attitude manifested in many textbooks on method which come close to being textbooks on statistics and which, while not condemning other methods, suggest that they are but poor relatives and only to be used in default of access to the right ones.

It is the assertiveness of the Positivist tradition which leads to a strong reaction against it; a reaction that is, often, equally excessive. It is the kind of reaction which is likely to present qualitative work as though it were a crusade regarding Positivism as not just mistaken but evil, oppressive, and dehumanising, seeking to reduce all human relations to quantitative terms. To such critics Positivism appears as the intellectual extension of the bureaucratic spirit at its bleakest and most insensitivie. But why does Positivism take such an imperialistic turn? One reason is that it is more than a methodological doctrine, it is also a philosophical one, and one with a very iconoclastic disposition. Its main target is other philosophical positions. In many ways it aims at putting itself forward as the last philosophical position advancing the cause of 'positive science' as the only bona fide source of knowledge against the claims of metaphysics and theology. It wants to argue, in effect, that science has replaced philosophy and that there is only one kind of knowledge, namely, that acknowledged by science. Positivism is a crusade against pretenders to knowledge and it is this which leads to the dismissive attitude discussed above. Those methods which do not fit the Positivist prescription cannot be sources of knowledge since, by its terms, there can only be one kind of knowledge, and that acquired by the methods of empirical science.

Positivists also believe in the unity of science: that there can be only one kind of knowledge and, hence, there cannot be any principled difference between the natural and the social sciences. What they share are the same methods. The methods of natural science are characterised by, first, the use of mathematical and quantitative procedures and, second, formal logically deductive theory. This second characteristic of natural science, at least as seen by Positivists, is concerned with the construction of explicit theoretical systems which generate hypotheses, or predictions, about the nature of the world. The link between the theories and the world is provided by the testing of hypotheses. Hence research is done in the service of theory and is only of use if it tests a theory's hypotheses.

So, in essence, the Positivist position comes down to the uncompromising view that unless something can be stated in mathematical or logical symbolism it is virtually not worth saying. It finds its expression in the assertion oft quoted that 'if it can't be measured it doesn't exist' and in the argument that most of what passes for theory in sociology is not theory at all because it does not take the form of a logically organised, deductively related, symbolically stated scheme of hypotheses.

We are not suggesting that all who favour Positivism in sociology take the extreme position we have outlined here. Nevertheless, stated boldly it enables us to draw out what a criticism of Positivism needs to claim. It need not claim to refute it decisively, arguing that there is nothing at all to be said for Positivism, only to present a reasoned rejection of its claim to exclusivity. As far as sociological method is concerned, this would make room for qualitative methods wherever they may be suitably employed, and also occasions the possibility of appraising research on its individual merits rather than on some general and extrinsic criterion such as the kind of methodology employed. Arguing, in sum, that there is no reason why those who employ qualitative methods should, at this time, accept the position of 'poor relatives' to those doing surveys or testing hypotheses, or using quantitative methods.

In arguing against positions like Positivism it is often best to proceed by a two-step strategy and to begin by granting the opposition as much of their case as possible. That is, give it as much as can reasonably be granted of what is claimed and then see if the case will stand up. It is often the case that one finds, on inspection, that a great deal less is being conceded than first appears and that even when considerable allowance is made for the opposition case it still does not have enough to justify its stronger, and more interesting, claims. Once this has been done, we may begin to doubt the assumptions that have been allowed; the debatable contentions that have, for argument's sake, been granted.

There is no need to begin, then, with the assumption that Positivism is morally outrageous, if not criminal. Let us grant that there is much to be said for Positivism's main contentions about the appropriate sociological method. Let us also assume that, other things being equal, we should prefer quantitative material and results to the qualitative kind and that an explicitly formulated, logically deductive theory is better than a discursive account in ordinary language. Let us accept these for much the same reasons that are often given in their support. If we are seeking to identify variables and if we can specify these in quantitative terms and measure them accurately, then it is likely that we shall be able to settle questions much more efficiently than if we cannot.

A great deal of sociology is rather like the situation after election nights: whatever the result all parties can take some satisfaction from the outcome. A way of intepreting the result which will show that a party's position is better than it might have been can always be found. Similarly, in sociology many of the disputes about empirical matters seem to arise because there is no precise way of assessing the relevant facts. In regard to poverty, for example, have things got better or worse since the Second World War? If we had a generally accepted way of measuring poverty a question such as this could be more easily settled. We could see whether there is worse poverty now than then, how much improvement, if any, there has been, and so on. Accordingly, we see no reason to dispute the claim that many similar disputes in the discipline could be more intelligently conducted if we could quantify the relevant factors.

Likewise much can be said on behalf of deductive theory. If we have a logically explicit theory in which the various propositions are spelt out and clearly related, where words are replaced by symbols which are manipulated according to strict rules, then empirical sociology would make substantial gains. For one thing we should have to spend less time trying to make out just what it is the theories say. As we have already indicated, one of the great difficulties which attends any attempt to say whether Marx or Weber or Durkheim is right or wrong is that of making out what they did say. Further, even when one has a reasonably acceptable version of their position it is not, by any means, an automatic next step to see whether their theory hangs together. There are all kinds of ways of ordering what they have to say, and something, which, from one angle, looks incoherent, from another can appear less so. Add to all this the fact that even when we have established something like an acceptable and coherent theory, we still do not have something which is so clear that we can tell what it would take to show that it is wrong or not.

We can agree, too, that if we can express our ideas in a logico-mathematical way, then we have at our disposal the power of developed mathematical techniques to get much more out of our theories than we do at present. A formal theory makes implications both more unequivocal and apparent. There is less room for doubt as to what follows from what and a much greater opportunity to see if the theory leads to surprising conclusions. For example, the idea that the speed of light is the ultimate speed beyond which it is impossible to go is one which gains much of its force from the fact that Einstein's theory is stated mathematically, some of the equations showing that the velocity of anything else must work out at less than the speed of light. This strange and difficult idea is made apparent through the mathematics: without them it might not have been so readily seen, if appreciated at all. We grant, then, that it might be possible for sociology to be unified with natural science, to have the same kind of methods, and that it would be desirable for it to follow this path.

So, having conceded these quite debatable points have we achieved very much in solving sociology's present problems? Have we accepted that there is no choice but to set about implementing the Positivist programme? If so, what does it take to do this?

From the point of view of sociology, the first problem that emerges is that there is nothing specifically sociological about the Positivist programme. The arguments apply to sociology only by virtue of the fact that it applies to any science. The Positivist programme tells us only that the kinds of methods to be used must be the same as those used in the natural sciences. What it does not do is tell us how they are to be used and what they are to be used for. Far from being a solution to sociology's problems it apears to be a restatement of them: sociology is a discipline in which it is hard to say things in a clear and unambiguous way, more than difficult to know what evidence would settle disputed questions, and so on. This is the problem and urging that we express theories in unambiguous symbols, state problems in such a way that relevant and decisive data are identifiable and obtainable does not take us far towards its solution. It is rather like saying that there is an energy crisis but that this can be resolved if we have a source of cheap, non-polluting, and easily obtained energy. This would indeed resolve the crisis, but we have the crisis because we do not have such a source, nor are we near to obtaining one.

A second issue is that Positivism's claim to superiority in sociology is not based on its track record in the discipline. Its claim on sociology arises from the success of the programme in other disciplines which does not ensure that it will prove equally viable in sociology. The mere fact that quantitative methods have accomplished far more elsewhere does not justify claims for the pre-eminence of quantification in contemporary sociology, and it is a moot point, as far as sociology is concerned, whether they have managed anything more than the qualitative methods they despise.

At this stage we are not disputing the terms of the Positivist argument but accepting them pretty much as given. In this spirit, then, it is reasonable to attempt to assess its achievements not as they would look from a quantitative outlook but in their own terms: by its own standards, how well is Positivist sociology doing? Positivism is stern and what is sauce for the goose is sauce for the gander. Positivism in criticism of other approaches delivers harsh judgements and it is only fair, then, that its standards be applied with equal vigour to work done under its auspices, and it is to this we now turn.

Positivism lays its stress on the use of quantification and logical expression and the question is what do these involve? Putting numbers and logical symbols down on a page, filling up papers with statistical tables, equations, computer print-outs, and mathematical models is not the same as being quantitative and logical. Mathematics and logic, like games, have rules and very strict ones, tougher and more demanding than we are likely to meet elsewhere. So, to be quantitative and logical one must play by the rules of mathematics and logic otherwise one does not simply make mistakes but fails to play at all. It is much more than a matter of just using mathematical and logical symbols but manipulating them according to the relevant rules. There is a great deal of difference between the genuine use of logic and mathematics and the mere imitation of them. Failure to stick to the strict requirements of the 'games', so to speak, is only to engage in a kind of mumbo-jumbo. Accordingly, it is not enough to make a superficial inspection of a piece of sociology to see if it contains number and logical symbols; it is necessary to scrutinise what it does with these in order to see whether they fulfil the requirements of logical and mathematical reasoning and are not just going through the motions.

Cicourel's book, *Method and Measurement in Sociology* examples the kind of damage which can be done to Positivist sociology by the strict application of its own criteria. Although Cicourel marshals arguments about the nature of natural language and its importance as the medium of social communication which could be used to suggest an in-principle objection to quantification in important areas of socio-logical study, it is not these kinds of objections he is aiming to make. He is not, in other words, arguing against the idea of a mathematical and quantitative sociology. Indeed, he is as much concerned as anyone might be with the question of how the cause of such a sociology might be advanced. He is, however, arguing against what passes for quantitiative work in sociology, maintaining that it does not typically meet the minimum requirements for proper measurement and mathematical inference.

Cicourel provides an exposition of what is known as the 'theory of measurement', which tries to spell out some of the ground rules of measurement and identify what assumptions must be satisfied in order to claim that one is measuring something. These assumptions set stiff standards. Too stiff, Cicourel argues, to be satisfied by current sociological research practices. Measuring something is more than just a matter of sticking numbers on to things in arbitrary ways. To make genuine measurements we have to know a great deal already about the things we intend to investigate, the things being measured, and the things being used as measuring instruments. For example, to make a thermometer work as a measure of temperature we have to know about the relationship between increases in temperature and the rate of expansion of a substance such as mercury. We can use mercury thermomenters to measure temperature because we know that there is a correspondence between the increase in temperature and the rate of expansion of the metal. That is, we can make strong assumptions about the correspondence between properties of the measurement scale, in this case temperature, and the properties of the material to which it is applied. Theory of measurement, then, tells us, among other things, about the need to be able to assume 'isomorphism' between scale and phenomenon.

However, it is not just a matter of making measurements but making ones which can be manipulated mathematically. There are different levels of measurement and not all lend themselves equally to mathematical operations. For example, while rank order measures allow us to place objects in some order, such as 'this is bigger than that', 'this came first, that second', 'this exhibits more of X than that', we cannot do very much with them by way of calculation, which is, of course, one of the points of using numbers. But, if we can rank objects in a 'stronger' way, such that we can say that this is twice the size of that, four times the size of the other, and so on, that is, quantify the relation between the items on the scale, then we can start to use the basic mathematical operations of additon, subtraction, multiplication, and division. Unfortunately, in sociological studies it is not all that easy to give such strong rankings to the phenomena under investigation.

Consider coding responses to a questionnaire. The responses can be given numerical values. Thus, an 'agree' response to some statement can be given a score of 1 and a 'strongly agree' a score of 5. What cannot be assumed is that the feeling expressed by 'strongly agree' is five times as strong as that expressed by 'agree'. Expressions of feeling, or attitude, towards something, whether it be the present government, Arthur Scargill, one's partner, the weather, or whatever, are not invariant with respect to either persons or the occasions on which the feeling is expressed. Admittedly, some kind of numbering can be done but only of the weakest kind, and certainly not the kind which allows mathematical manipulation of the kind we can use on measurements of, say, length. All we are justified in saying, mathematically speaking, in the example just used is that X's feelings are stronger (about some matter) than Y's

So, although we can give numerical values to things we have to ask ourselves whether, having done so, we are better off. Would we be worse off in terms of our understanding of the things we want to study if we used letter rather than numerical codes: if we classify 'agree' as A and 'strongly agree' as E are we losing any essential information?

Perhaps the numerical scoring helps in putting the data into computers, but the fact that we are using numbers here carries no extra informational value, has no sociological significance. In giving numbers of this kind we cannot take advantage of the virtues quantification is supposed to bring within our reach.

Cicourel's criticism of experimental method in social science is similar. Again, it originates in a consideration of the conventionally conceived goals and requirements of the experimental method. The method is aimed at the specification of the relationship between variables by the control and simplification of the situation to minimise the effects of extraneous factors. Cicourel alleges that the use of the method in sociology is little more than a ritual trapping. There is little real effort to control variables and, in any case, insufficient knowledge of the kinds of things that ought to be controlled without which what are called experiments are so in name only. Cicourel does not object to the idea that experiments might be used in sociology, but points out the obligations we incur if we try to make genuine experiments rather than emulating the empty forms of laboratory practice.

Cicourel is well known as an Ethnomethodologist and though his arguments do not hinge upon acceptance of this particular viewpoint it might be thought, none the less, that Cicourel's case is partisan and, in any event, now twenty years out of date. To show that the passage of time has not invalidated what Cicourel has to say and also demonstrate that one does not have to be an Ethnomethodologist to see that quantitative work faces serious difficulties, it is worth quoting from the much more recent writings of Blalock, a leading protagonist of quantitative sociology. In writing of the 'trade-offs' between generalisability, simplicity, and precision, he identifies a fundamental dilemma for the social scientist:

> Although it is obviously desirable, in the abstract, to strive for theories that are simultaneously parsimonious, highly general, and therefore applicable to a wide range of phenomena, yet precise enough to imply rejectable hypotheses, it does not appear possible within the social sciences to achieve simultaneously all three of these ideal characteristics.

He goes on to draw the conclusion that a more serious attitude to the development of genuine measurement is called for, one which takes a critical attitude to much so-called measurement and faces up to the serious difficulties involved.

> We must become accustomed to the much more tedious process of trying to make as precise theoretical distinctions as we can, and examining carefully what each of these implies about measurement. We then must

learn to state explicitly just what assumptions are required in going from the theoretical constructs to operational procedures, the conditions under which these assumptions are most likely to be realistic, and the modifications that may be needed to extend the measurement to other settings.

An important implication of Cicourel's line of argument is that there is no intrinsic merit to research methods as such. There is no particular virtue in putting things in numerical form, nor in choosing the experiment, or the social survey because these facilitate some primitive counting and the use of statistical analysis. The issue is not one of choosing between quantitative and qualitative methods, but learning to discriminate between good and bad quantitative work and good and bad qualitative work. It suggests, too, that the standard against which the quality of research is appraised be shifted away from that of formal compliance with the abstract requirements of a particular kind of research towards a much more means–ends oriented assessment of it: Does this research succeed in achieving the ends it has set for itself? Does it, could it, do what it aims to do in this way? Does it even come close? And so on.

Much the same kind of argument can be directed against that other component of the Positivist programme, the hypothesis-testing method. Once again, there is no reason to suggest that it would not be a useful way of organising sociological research. Hypotheses could be put forward, the relevant data collected, and the hypothesis subjected to a searching test. However, there is a question mark that needs to be put against the treatment of the steps involved in the standard hypothesis-testing method as though they represented the nature of effective sociological research as such, or as if the following of them would lead automatically to better sociological work.

The first point to make is that the hypothesis-testing method is not an end in itself. The point of research organised in this way is not simply to test hypotheses. The real rationale for a hypothesis-testing strategy, as we have pointed out, lies in the requirement for logically explicit, deductive theory. The theory should make specific, preferably quantifiable, empirical predictions which make it possible to test the theory as a whole. If we can derive from a theory some prediction which will have a decisive relation to the theory as a whole, some prediction which if it is wrong must cast the basic principles of the theory into doubt, then testing hypotheses has some point. The research, the test, in other words tells for or against the theory. Anyone can cook up loads of testable hypotheses. But the random composition of arbitrarily conjured up hypotheses is of no scientific interest whatsoever. It is only in association with serious theory building that the hypothesis-testing method takes on a useful role. Accordingly, the question is what can Positivism offer as guidance towards the production of genuine theory?

Much the same arguments apply here as were given in respect of quantitative method. Just putting ideas in the form of a deductive theory, writing them down using logical symbols, does not constitute theory construction. The Positivist criteria concern how things are said and do not help much with the issue of what is said. The logical form of a deductive scheme can easily be mapped out; it is something else altogether to produce some sociologically significant content to occupy that form. Although we could try to express the theories we have more formally, the question is whether this would be worth our while. Would it add anything to the theory? Would it improve it or merely be an exercise in translating it from one kind of expression to another? It is not enough to show that a theory could be deductively expressed, what needs to be shown is that it is substantially improved thereby. If nothing substantial is added by reformulating the theory in this way, then all that has been shown, contrary to Positivist claims, is that we do as well without adopting their methods as we do by taking them up. It may be, for example, that to achieve such reformulation we shall divest the theory of much of its current significance. One of the advanatages of formal expression is that it requires us to strip matters down to their barest minimum and, by doing so, hope that we produce something simple, spare yet powerful. Yet, there is no guarantee that we will find that all the important things we want to say can be so boiled down; that is, in reducing things to their absolute essentials we may find that we have to eliminate much that is valuable. So, stating sociological theories in formal terms we may find that we have to 'force' them into such a scheme divesting them of such virtues as they have without compensating gains.

The dilemma facing those who aim at quantitative work and formal theory is between saying something which satisfies the requirements of the theory of measurement or the rules of formal deductive argument, and saying something which is of sociological interest and consequence. Thus, we can often find that the techniques of quantification and formal reasoning far outrun the requiremens of sociology. Many of the contributions to the Positivist programme consist either in expositions of the available mathematical and logical techniques available or in 'exercises' with those resources. Thus, books on mathematical sociology tend to have much more about mathematics in them than sociology. In so far as they do have sociological work in them this is not done as mathematical sociology but as an exercise in applying mathematics to sociological materials to show what could be done if the right sort of data or theory was available.

None of the objections reviewed above deny the general validity of the Positivist position. There are arguments which aim to do this and there are sociologists who think the kind of difficulties and dilemmas we have just pointed to, and others, are intrinsic to the Positivist programme and not just a feature of early efforts to apply it within sociology. Just for the record, let us indicate these objections. Broadly they are of two main types. First, those which argue that the Positivist idea of the nature of science is misleading, if not badly distorted, in failing to understand the part which mathematical and logical expressions play in the sciences where they are most deeply ingrained. Such expressions depend upon much which is neither quantified nor logically regimented. Like any body of knowledge, science exists within a fiduciary framework which serves as a foundation determining the direction in which it proceeds and the acceptability of its explanations. In a word, science is built upon presuppositions. Second, those which argue that the requiremens of Positivist method are imcompatible with a genuine understading of human beings and their social lives. That is, the development of mathematical and quantitiative sociology can only proceed at the expense of understanding and that we shall invariably have to remove sociologically interesting content in order to contain ideas within a logico-mathematical framework.

As we have said before, we do not think that such in-principle arguments are necessary to achieve the important objective, namely, to justify the argument that Positivism has no special claim on sociologists' attentions and efforts at the present time. It shares with other approaches the generic problems of the discipline. Positivism is not a solution to sociology's problems. Like other positions, it is a proposal, an agenda, about the direction in which a solution may be sought. Its plight is just as problematical as is that of anti-Positivist traditions, not less so. Indeed, many of its problems are not peculiar to it, as we have said, but are generic to the discipline, and which have to do with creating good ideas and designing effective studies. Because of its emphasis on the way in which things are said, the formal requirements, at the expense of a concern for what can be said with them, Positivism has not much devoted itself to creating ideas about social organisation which could provide the stuff of any formal theory. In consequence, Positivism's sociological ideas are just about as good or as bad as anyone else's; in fact, in large part are much the same as anyone else's. The sociological problem which faces it is the same one that faces all of us, that we do not rest content with received ideas but try to improve on them to get a better understanding, sociologically speaking, of the social world. However, the quantitative researcher's problems are, perhaps, doubly difficult. They must not only create good sociological ideas but must also be ideas which can, without serious loss, be put into mathematical terms, laid out in a deductive theory, and related to genuine measurement scales. No small task.

Likewise with the generic problem we identified, that is, producing effective studies which work out. All sociologists, if they set themselves anything other than the simplest problems, have real difficulties identifying the right kind of data that will enable them to answer the problems they have set, have difficulties in obtaining such data, and no little trouble in making them do what they want them to do if they can be obtained. And these difficulties beset both qualitative and quantitative research.

QUANTITATIVE VERSUS QUALITATIVE?

As we said at the beginning of this chapter, the dispute about methods in sociology is generally seen as a battle between two opposing forces, the 'quantitative' and the 'qualitative', as if these were sets of methods which are both sharply distinguished and necessarily opposed. However, the distinction between the two is not as sharp as is often made out. In any science, no matter how quantitative, qualitative elements are thoroughly involved, in, for example, making judgements about what measurements imply, deciding how to classify the data, assigning a metric to the instances to be quantified, gauging the significance of findings, and so on. Correspondingly, there are quantitative elements in qualitative work, such as making judgements about the relative frequency of some event, the likelihood of some occurrence, the importance of some factor, and so on. Nevertheless, there is some animus between researchers of the different kinds. There is a catalogue of terms which is frequently used to identify each method: the qualitative one is 'soft', 'descriptive', 'speculative', 'relativistic', 'exploratory', and 'subjective', while the quantitative one is 'hard', 'explanatory', 'rigorous', 'objective', and so on. These are virtues or vices depending upon your point of view: quantitative researchers often pride themselves on being 'hard-nosed' but their qualitative critics see this as just what is wrong with them.

It looks, then, as if there is a real choice here, real dilemmas for research. If you want to be 'hard', 'rigorous', and 'objective' in your research then you should use the social survey or some other quantitative technique, or if you want to do field-work then you must accept that it cannot be as rigorous but 'merely' subjective and soft.

There is certainly a long-standing association between the respective methods and various other 'hard' and 'soft' attitudes. Thus, we tend to find that those who favour quantitative methods will want to take a 'hard-nosed' attitude to the study of human beings: they will allow no loose talk about 'subjective meanings' or any sentimental ideas about taking a sympathetic attitude to the people they study. Their 'hard-nosed' attitude also permeates their view of the need for objectivity consisting, in the most extreme cases, of an almost literal application of the word: objectivity consists in treating human beings as objects, seeing no difference between them and any other kind of object, and, naturally, refusing to see any need for special ways of researching into them. Qualitative researchers are often disposed to accept and share these ideas about what makes for 'hard' research and objective work and, thus, to denigrate such objectives. Their work is subjective, concerned to show recognition of other human beings as human beings, as creatures different from other kinds of objects and with which they have a special bond. Not only are they not going to force their research into moulds that quantitative strategies impose, but are not going to impose any kinds of restraints upon it; they will express their own subjectivity, do their work as the spirit moves them and however it moves them.

However, although the association of these attitudes with the respective methods is long-established, there is no necessary connection between them. We do not have to adopt some sort of empiricist or behaviouristic doctrines because we want to use quantitative methods or resign all pretensions to rigour just because we want to employ qualitative ones. It is always useful to remind ourselves that before coming to any choice we should look to see if the options available are the only ones to be had. In this case, as in so many others, it seems to us that they are not. As a matter of fact, one of the areas of the human sciences in which mathematics and formal theorising have made the greatest impact is in the study of language, particularly through Chomsky's 'transformational generative grammar': a contribution from a position which is determinedly and extremely anti-behaviourist. It styles itself 'mentalist' to indicate just how far it is from behaviourism. Things 'of the mind', so to speak, can be investigated with mathematical and other formal techniques. Though the available quantitative policies in sociology could not investigate 'subjective meanings', for example, very satisfactorily at the present time, this does not mean that 'subjective meanings' are intrinsically inaccessible to quantitative inquiry.

Nor is there any justification for seeing an essential dissociation of qualitative techniques and rigour. There is nothing particularly rigorous about the use of quantitative methods in ways that violate the rules that govern their use. 'Rigour' is not a characteristic of instruments but of the way in which they are employed. If rigour is to be sought in sociology it is to be sought in the reasoning, in the care with which this is done, in the thought that implements the research procedures, that chooses them and applies them with thoroughness and scruple, in the analysis which is made of the data and the tightness with which evidence and inference are related. Although mathematics and logic can be of great assistance in achieving rigour, they are not its constituents. Qualitative research can show a concern for the integrity of its inquiries which can match that of the other kind. Zoologists, for example, use 'naturalistic' methods of the kind that are often called for in sociology to study animals in their natural habitats; a tendency which has made positive gains in the rigour of zoological work even though much of it has produced qualitative descriptions of animal behaviour.

Arguments can also be developed in connection with 'objectivity'. There is often a conflation of two quite different senses of the word, such that the objectivity of findings, that is, that they are not merely matters of opinion or prejudice but have value independently of the preferences of those who produce them, is often gratuitously identified with the idea of viewing everything as though it were an object. Qualitative research can be organised so that the collection, recording, and presentation of data are largely independent of personal preferences and the use of tape and video recorders in this connection can produce data which are as hard as any data could be. Further, interpreting and analysing quantitative materials as carefully and as thoughtfully as possible does not make it unworthy of the epithet 'objective'. Of course, qualitative researchers may take the view that there is more to life than rigour and objectivity and if they are right in thinking that what they want can only be had at the cost of pursuing rigour and objectivity, then so be it. Our point is that qualitative researchers do not have to take the view that their research is doomed to be soft and subjective just because it is qualitative.

The conflict between quantitative and qualitative research can be seen as another instance of the way in which some disputes in sociology, often philosophical in character but not invariably so, and their solution, are treated as preliminaries to research itself. Sort these out and research will, more or less, take care of itself. But, as we have stressed, empirical research, of whatever kind, is not easy to do properly even assuming resolution of disputes such as this. Nevertheless, the dispute about methods is, in our view, unnecessarily principled. What it virtually implies is that method should dictate the phenomena and the problems that are investigated rather than the other way around. As a dispute it seeks to lay down what kind of phenomena can be legitimately studied independently, and prior to, the effort of studying them and facing up to the problems so revealed.

We have argued elsewhere in this book that a 'problem-centred' approach to what is needed in sociology could be of considerable benefit, and no more so than in the area of method. Methods ought to be chosen in light of the problem rather than vice versa. The methods available to any discipline are not canonical forms of inquiry but only stocks of methods in hand and no reason why their number should not be increased, or decreased, as problems dictate. The appropriate role for methods in sociology is to assist in the investigation of sociological problems, and it is this which should be the appropriate yardstick to use in their appraisal. As we have also suggested before, the methods of natural science have been very successful, but this does not make them definitive of the methods of scientific inquiry in general. It remains to be seen if they can be as successful in deepening our understanding of the nature of human life as they have been in natural scientific inquiries. The attitude expressed by Feyerabend is not inappropriate in this connection. He argues that in scientific work attachment to the idea that there is a set of definitive methods for science is a chronic form of intellectual conservatism: a posture that, in effect, has ceased trying to understand matters that are puzzlng by ruling them out of consideration rather than facing up to them. We take Feyerabend's suggestion that 'anything goes' not as saying that it does not matter what is done in the name of science, but rather that there is no reason not to try something simply because a principled objection to it has been made. Many are attracted to the idea that there is a particular formula identifying successful science, or successful sociology, but no one has yet succeeded in formulating one which has received universal assent, or which fits unambiguously and accounts for the success of particular sciences.

So, in sum, the debate between quantitative and qualitative methods as usually conducted is largely a sterile one in our view. It does not have to be solved in any principled way, which is not to say that there are no problems with either kind of method, to proceed with empirical work. Both sides represent proposals for sociological inquiry and, as such, are both legitimate and respectable. What they do not have to be is proposals for restricting sociological interests. Carrying both in harness as possible ways for sociology to proceed still leaves us with many problems, many puzzles, many difficulties, but this is, as we have urged before, part of the ongoing argumentative life of the discipline.

RESEARCH AND SOCIOLOGICAL PERSPECTIVES

Although at the beginning of this book we cast doubt, on a number of scores, on the perspectives metaphor as a way of organising sociological ideas, there is another set of issues, and bewilderments, which are worth dealing with in some detail, namely, the relationship between empirical research and sociological perspectives.

The frequent complaint about the 'gap' between theory and research in sociology has much to do with the way in which, despite lip-service to the contrary, theorising and research are regarded as largely autonomous pursuits. In this respect the present situation is not all that different from C W Mills' characterisation of some years ago. He found two sets of dissociated activities in sociology: 'grand theory' and 'abstracted empiricism'. The former involved the creation of would-be comprehensive, abstract, and speculative theoretical schemes, spinning out their logical interconnections without much thought for whether or not they made contact with the empirical world. The latter, though empirical, was conducted without much regard for the theoretical significance of the studies, their purpose, and their relationship to each other.

We take it that the ideal relationship between theory and research is one in which theoretical problems are answered by research, and research projects established for their potential theoretical significance. Theory should explain, organise, and integrate knowledge so as to give reasonably clear directions for research. Research should not just accumulate information but collect data that will count as answers to questions posed by theory. Theory, research, and one should add, research methods and techniques, are not ends in themselves but require each other to do their job in improving our sociological understanding of society and social life. Instead what we find, briefly, is that theory exceeds its empirical relevance, methods their research utility, and research its theoretical import. The gaps abound and we do not suppose, any more than with other issues we have raised, that there is an easy way of closing them. There are deeply rooted reasons why sociology has such gaps, including features of its own organisation, which perpetuate them. But, above all, the reasons are to do with the very serious difficulties involved in formulating good theories, assembling effective research, and putting together bodies of data. Perhaps all that it is possible to recommend at this stage is that sociologists need to exhibit a greater concern for the ends–means relationship in theory and research.

There is, however, a particularly unhelpful way of thinking about the relation between theory and research which we have already mentioned in this chapter, namely, research as a 'hypothesis-testing process'. On this characterisation the researcher is seen as beginning with a carefully framed hypothesis as to what, under particular conditions, is the expected relationship between two or more variables. The relevant data are collected and compared with the hypothesis' predictions, so refuting or confirming it. But, as we said earlier, it is a process for testing theories not hypotheses. Hypotheses have their interest in the theories from which they originate and, accordingly, require for their proper test a well-developed research methodology, some fairly exact theories providing specific and unambiguous predictions, and precise research designs allowing for the isolation of relevant evidence, its reliable recording, and the control of irrelevant factors. Without these, hypothesis testing is a fruitless exercise. Moreover, if the hypothesis-testing method is an idealisation of scientific research generally, it is a travesty of what passes for sociological research which tends to follow the following patterns. A researcher will begin with a diffuse idea about some topic and then collect whatever material seems relevant. A participant observer may choose a particular community or setting for research, but what is observed is dictated as much by the pattern of life found there as it is by any theoretical considerations. The survey schedule may look like a systematically designed and highly controlled procedure, but it is by no means unknown for its design principle to be little more than asking about as many things as possible within a manageable length. Further, it is often after the survey data have been collected that the researcher begins to frame hypotheses; the data themselves are not the result of some hypothesis-testing procedure.

Sociological approaches are rightly called 'perspectives' in that they are not so much collections of logically interrelated propositions and hypotheses, but consist mainly of recommendations as to 'ways of looking' or 'points of view'. What this implies about the place of empirical research can be illustrated by an example of research using 'labelling theory', itself an application of the Symbolic Interactionist perspective.

Labelling theory asks us to look at deviant actions as phenomena produced by the interactions between those who are classed as 'deviant' and those who are not. More specifically, it proposes that deviance be seen as the result of a labelling process which signifies how those labelled as deviant in some way are treated by others. Deviance, to put it simply, is a social creation; it is 'made' by social actors. A good example is Lemert's research on paranoia. A paranoid is one who feels conspired against. In psychiatric terms the paranoid is a person who has an unreasonable and unrealistic fear of persecution. Lemert argues, however, that from the point of view of the person labelled as paranoid such fears are neither unreasonable nor unrealistic. He is being 'persecuted' even though those who 'conspire' against him see themselves as acting in his best interests and concerned that he is becoming mentally ill. They lie to him, conceal and organise things behind his back, talk about him surreptitiously, make attempts to manipulate and control him, and so on. Naturally, the 'conspiracy' draws attention to itself and further confirms the paranoid's fears. Seen in this light, the paranoid's behaviour exhibits a sensitive and rational appreciation of what is going on around him. The conspiratorial activities of others puts him increasingly in an uncomfortable position, one in which his attempts to restore matters are likely to make things worse by simply confirming the label placed upon him. Such efforts are not seen as efforts of a normal person to explain or redeem the opinion others have of him, but, given the label, yet further symptoms of his deteriorating state. He is pushed into a corner and the frustrated outbursts yet further confirm that something is wrong and that he requires medical treatment.

The point of research such as this is that it is difficult to understand quite what is meant by labelling theory's claim that deviance is 'made', is a social construction, in advance of such a study. It would be hard to describe the kinds of things people would do, the kind of actions they would perform, which would count as 'producing' deviance in others. A study such as Lemert's shows how the ideas of labelling theory can be 'filled out' by demonstrating their application to this case and how they might apply to other cases. The study, in short, makes a case for the approach to which it is related. It tries to show how a general strategy can be related to instances and that at least some things can be seen in its terms. It also provides evidential support by showing that there is some evidence for the perspective with which the theory is affiliated, there are some facts which fit the suggestions of the theory. What the research is not is some hypothesis-testing process as this is classically understood. Nor does it rule out alternative theories to those of labelling theory and its home, Symbolic Interactionalism.

Where it seems that we have to choose between 'ways of seeing', so to speak, it is possible to find an approach persuasive because it has evidential support. We *can* see the world in its terms. Unfortunately, as far as sociology is concerned, this overlooks the reasons why the choice arises in the first place. Of course the world can be seen through a perspective, but it can equally well be seen through others. They each produce evidence for their point of view. They can, with a little interpretation, take note of and sometimes incorporate, or explain away, facts which appear to go against them. Research supporting a particular perspective need not show that it supports this point of view better than the others available. Sociological data especially, require a good deal of interpretation to make them say anything at all. Indeed, it is the perspective, the point of view, the approach, which is drawn upon to interpret the data. The data are understood as supporting the position because they are interpreted through lenses, so to speak, furnished by the position. We can, for example, find evidence, though not necessarily the same evidence, to support the view that Britain is a stable and consensual society or that it is riven by conflicts of various kinds. But the task that eludes us is how to 'total' the evidence, as it were, to give a final judgement one way or the other. How the evidence for each is assembled is through reading or interpreting the facts in particular ways. A high frequency of strikes, for example, can be read as evidence for growing social unrest or as evidence of the way in which people can exercise their freedoms within a broad consensus on values. In its turn, the consensus over values can be interpreted as an agreement manipulated by the powerful, through the media and other institutions, to divert attention away from the sources of conflict within society. Facts in complex cases such as these come nowhere near 'speaking for themselves' and the reading they receive is heavily dependent upon the assumptions a researcher takes on board. The fact that data can be brought under the purview of a particular approach does not mean that they cannot be brought under that of another, or that a researcher has tried to account for them in alternative ways. Interpreting data in one way does not demonstrate that this way is superior: it merely confirms that it is a way of interpretation.

Once again we seem to have drifted perilously close to suggesting that anything goes in sociology since there would seem to be no principled way of choosing between points of view, perspectives, or in our metaphor 'games', least of all by using the 'facts of the matter' for these, too, are matters of interpretation. However, what we have said earlier in this book should show that this charge is misplaced. And as far as research is concerned, even though it is not hypothesis testing in the classic sense, it can be rigorous and systematic. The amount of freedom in the interpretation of sociological data does not imply that there is total freedom to have things any way a researcher wishes. No researcher can simply wish the world to be as his or her theory requires, or invent data to fit. As the game metaphor emphasises, designing sociology 'games', making them 'playable' as procedures for saying something sociological about the world, means that the rules that are devised, whether they be theories or techniques of investigation, as self-imposed constraints have to be followed as best we can. Not that this guarantees success. As we saw with Positivism, applying its 'rules' is a very hard and a very difficult business with as yet, in our view, very little to show.

Once again, the business comes back to setting out the arguments and interpretations as clearly as possible. A case has to be made for looking at the facts in whatever way we choose. It is difficult to make sociological data decide between approaches, and nor should we expect them to. The very loose connections between approaches, theories, techniques, and research in sociology do not allow data to be used in this way to any effect. But, at this stage of sociology's progress, as we have repeatedly stressed, we do not have to choose among the approaches or, the subject of this chapter, methods, as exclusive proposals for the way the discipline is to conceptualise its phenomena and conduct its empirical research. Whether it will always be this way is too early to say. This is the way it is at the moment. This still leaves much to be done, problems to solve, puzzles to work out, arguments to review, not least to do with enhancing the connections between theory, methods, and research.

FURTHER READING

T W ADORNO *et al.*, *The Positivist Dispute in German Sociology*, Heinemann, 1976.   An expression of the disagreement with Positivism especially as a 'dehumanising' force.

H BLALOCK, *Conceptualisation and Measurement*, Sage, 1982. A good example of the problems posed by quantification as seen by someone committed to this approach. The quotations in the text are to be found on pp. 27–8 and 31 respectively.

A V CICOUREL, *Method and Measurement in Sociology*, Free Press,

1964. Still vital after twenty years.

W J FILSTEAD, *Qualitative Sociology*, Markham, 1970. Contains papers dealing with many aspects of qualitative research. Especially the papers by Becker and Blumer.

P HALFPENNY, *Positivism and Sociology*, Allen and Unwin, 1983. A more discriminating account of the variety of Positivism.

G C HOMANS, *The Nature of Social Science*, Harcourt Brace, 1967. A classic, brief, vigorous, and aggressive statement of Positivism.

E LEMBERT, 'Paranoia and the dynamics of exlusion', *Sociometry*, 25, 1962. See pp.2–25 for the study referred to in the text.

J LYONS, *Chomsky*, Fontana, 1970. A relatively simple account of Chomsky's ideas.

C W MILLS, *The Sociological Imagination*, Penguin, 1970. A still refreshing commentary on the state of sociology.

Chapter 7
READING SOCIOLOGY: GOFFMAN AS EXAMPLE

In part, this chapter will go over and re-emphasise what we hope are, by now, some very familiar themes. In addition, we will take this opportunity to pick out one important and largely neglected aspect of the introduction necessary to sociology. Crucial to the development of sociological awareness and competence is learning to read sociology. In our view, this involves coming to see sociological work as the exercise of sociological reasoning. This is an argument which we have been trying to make and support throughout this book. We have chosen to illustrate just what it might mean by referring to the work of Erving Goffman. There are many reasons for this. Goffman is extremely popular with both teachers and students. His books and papers have an easy-to-read character which at times belies their often difficult topic matter. They display an immediacy and vivacity which is probably only rivalled in the discipline by the ethnographic writings of Oscar Lewis and Clifford Geertz. But Goffman is also much misunderstood, or perhaps misapprehended would be better, since to judge from many of the critical commentaries on him, he strikes some people as shallow, without significance, his work espousing a cyncial attitude towards human nature, as well as being overly dependent on non-sociological sources and findings. It is thought to be 'impressionistic', riven by problems of inference and validity, and by no means a contribution to the development of an 'objective' social science. The primary test of this inadequacy is the sheer impossibility of replication. Goffman's contributions are unique, and illuminating and insightful though they might be, are in the end unscientific. Because of this, they cannot be taken as exemplars of sociological work. In our opinion, this estimation is wrong. If Goffman is read sociologically, his worth becomes apparent. This chapter will try to show why.

If there is one single lesson which we hope all those who read this book will draw from it, it is the acceptance of the often unappreciated fact that sociology is, by its very nature, a difficult disicpline. The reasons for this difficulty lie both in its topic matter and the methodological attitude involved. In trying to disguise the difficulty of the discipline, sociologists sometimes do it less than justice by setting ambitions for it which it is extremely unlikely to be able to achieve. The most obvious result of this underplaying of the difficulty and peculiarity of the discipline, and the problems it faces, is the familiar list of complaints that are made. It is long-winded and jargon ridden, replete with generalisations, and possessed of an overweening ambition and totally unfounded sense of its own importance. Its contributions, when not opaque to the point of mystification, appear doctrinaire and dogmatic. As Goffman himself has pointed out, more than one commentator has declared that they would swap the whole enterprise for a few good conceptual distinctions and a cold beer!

As we have said before, there is, unfortunately, more than a grain of truth in this unflattering estimation. However, it *is* an exaggeration. It is unjust, no matter how sympathetic one might be towards such an opinion. Some sociological research reporting does look as if it were designed deliberately to annoy those of a practical, pragmatic bent whose criteria of worth are cumulations of clear and precise findings directed towards some useful purpose, and communicated in simple and easy-to-understand ways. To the outsider, and the novice, a great deal of sociology is unsatisfactory when viewed in this light. None the less, this attiude is, we think, based upon a lack of appreciation not simply of the different sorts of sociological reasoning – or conventions of different sociological 'games', to use the image we have been employing – but also what to expect from and, hence, how to read sociology. The rest of this book has tried to explore the former. This chapter will take up the latter.

THE NATURE OF READING SOCIOLOGICALLY

What, then, do we mean when we say that people have to learn to read sociologically? What do they have to read sociology as and for? Naturally, there is no one answer to this. We have already seen that sociologists hold a variety of opinions on what the discipline should be and what it is committed to. C Wright Mills, for example, in a famous statement said that the prime object has to be the exploration of the relationship between private troubles and public issues. Without doubt, nearly everyone would have sympathy with the need perceived by Mills and the sentiments he expressed, even if we did not feel that sociology was best suited to the task nor the proper forum for such discussions. In similar vein, stung by Alvin Gouldner's critique of labelling theory, Howard Becker was adamant that the answer to the question 'Whose side are we on?' was unequivocal. Sociology, for him at least, had to be on the side of the underdog, those whose voices are rarely heard and who have little or no access to political and other resources. In contrast to what we might call a 'Tribune of the people' line, are those who prefer a more quietist approach. This might be exemplified by many who, while not necessarily denying the liberal and libertarian values of Gouldner, Mills and Becker do not feel that their sociological work has to fulfil them in quite this way. Some would want to promote 'scientific' objectivity as a prerequisite to what they view as 'piecemeal social engineering'. This is not the place to open up once more the debates surrounding these issues. All we want to point out is that these two clusters of sociologists propose different aspirations for the discipline. Further, we would also want to say that while it might be possible to distinguish tendencies such as the two mentioned, and they are by no means the only ones, they are not hard and fast. Many sociologists have done work that contributes to both traditions, Mills, Becker, and Gouldner are cases in point, and many more would want to resist any classificiation of their work in this way at all.

The first point to make, therefore, is that reading sociology means attempting to draw out the author's project. It means attending to individual pieces as instances of styles of sociological reasoning directed towards particular interests and ends. We have to be sensitive to the reasons why particular premises or departure points are chosen and how they have been defined, why specific data collection procedures have been selected, or ranges of argument marshalled and deployed. We have to try to see why inferences are thought to follow in the ways claimed and why the conclusions are drawn as they are. In short, we have to be prepared to become immersed in the 'game' being played and participate in it too. This is the second thing to emphasise. Reading sociologically means making the effort to understand why things have been done in the ways that are reported and how the arguments develop. It cannot mean categorising authors because of their interests and dismissing them and their work because those interests do not square with ours. Sociological reading requires an open-mindedness, a willingness to follow an argument through to the conclusion it reaches. None of this means, by any stretch of the imagination, that we think that all sociology rewards the expenditure of such effort equally. That is another matter entirely. No sociology will yield anything unless one is prepared to make some effort. Many of the objections, denigrations, and chortlings of those who object to the very existence of the discipline can be traced back to a wholesale refusal to make such an effort, or to be willing to grant that all sociological writings are examples of sociological reasoning in action.

The third theme which we have tried to develop in this book is the argumentative as opposed to discovery nature of the discipline. It consists of 'texts' making and countering arguments and positions. Even those forms of sociology which model themselves most closely on the natural sciences display this argumentative character. Grounds for the making of particular kinds of studies are displayed, links forged between the phenomena to be investigated and the measures used, the propriety of the methods for determining the degree of support the evidence gives the conclusions is defended. Part of the awareness of this argumentative character involves a reappraisal of the nature of investigative aims. What the arguments are about is not findings but the nature of the organisation of social life which the findings display. If we feel that the point is to make findings, then we are bound to be disappointed in those we have to hand. What sociology tells us about the origins of mental illnesses such as clinical depression, the nature of social problems such as crime and poverty, or work practices on automated production lines, appears to be little more than sophisticated versions of conventional wisdom. But it is not that the findings are produced that is the point of the exercise, but what is made of them. It is how we explain the findings, what arguments are proposed for their understanding and significance which is the heart of the matter.

Part of this sensitivity will involve an awareness of the import of different styles of sociological research reporting and writing. We can use format as a key to seeing what we are being invited to participate in. This means trying to understand the *logic* of the format; why for example, authors choose to present work in blocs sub-headed 'general problem', 'previous research', 'research design', 'findings', 'conclusions', 'discussion', and what might be gained and lost by using a different format. Using the format, though, should not be purely a mechanical matter. One of the great difficulties which a book like Talcott Parsons' *The Strucure of Social Action* presents for students is that it looks like a familiar, introductory survey of classical theorists, whereas it is, in fact, a highly idiosyncratic argument about Durkheim, Marshall, Pareto, Weber *et al*. Parsons is deliberately selective, and draws from their writings just what he wants. As we will see with Goffman in a moment, part of the point of the writing is carried by the format that is used.

But all this is very abstract and generalised. It needs to be tied down to specifics. Let us have a look at what a sociological reading of Goffman might involve.

READING ERVING GOFFMAN

The phenomenon under investigation

The difficulty that many people have in reading Goffman is not in understanding what he has to say, for his writing is a model of lucidity and panache. It is, rather, the feeling that Goffman ought to be saying something significant about human social life, but they cannot quite see what. They cannot make out what it all *adds up* to. What is its sociological significance? Granted the things he talks about are of intrinsic interest and that he often displays an astounding breadth of reading and illuminating insights into social relations, but none the less students especially are prone to feel that it is all an amorphous mass of unrelated pieces. It does not amount to a serious sociological project. Now it is true that reading Goffman for the very first time, one might come to this conclusion. He does range across an incredible diversity of social settings and sources, from the back-parlour of the hotel in the Shetlands to the casinos of Las Vegas, from books on etiquette and the novels of William Sansom to transcripts of television interviews and observations made of patients on the back-wards of mental hospitals. But through all of this material, in his use of all of these resources, there does run a constant theme. First and foremost, Goffman is concernd to describe what he himself calls 'the interaction order'; that is, the socially organised character of the behaviour of co-present selves. Throughout the many different topics and settings he takes up, this is a constant theme, even though it may be formulated in a variety of different ways and explored using numerous, alternative images. In each and every case, though, while the focus of attention shifts in level and may be more concentrated or diffuse, there is a similarity in the approach that is adopted. One has only to compare a series of his books to see how this is so.

The Presentation of Self in Everyday Life is quite obviously addressed to this theme, being concerned with selves as 'dramaturgical objects' giving and giving off impressions, just as actors give and give off impressions on the stage. And, just as we can talk of 'role performance', 'props', 'scenes', 'front-stage and back-stage' for the theatre, so we can use the same terms to capture aspects of our social lives. But the same direct concern with face-to-face interaction can be discerned in other works such as *Stigma*, *Frame Analysis*, and the rest, providing we allow ourselves to become sensitive to the variety of alternative *thematising devices* that Goffman uses to gain purchase on the collaborative nature of co-ordinated interaction.

Stigma has as its subtitle 'Notes on the management of spoiled identity'. This is a strong clue. It is not just about how we discriminate in daily life against cripples and the handicapped, ethnic groups, and social isolates. It is about how our treatment of these people is reacted to and managed by them. Our treatment projects upon them a 'spoiled identity', an incomplete 'virtual self' which, were it to be accepted would lead to the person so stigmatised accepting the label of non-normality. But, as Goffman indicates, this is precisely what does not happen. In a variety of ways, those who are stigmatised 'manage' this projection and so retain a self-conception of normality. Their 'management' strategies are as many and various as the people who put them into practice.

Frame Analysis looks to be a 'theoretical' book. It does not appear to be directed to some particular topic or set of situations. But, all the way through what Goffman is looking at is the familiar theme of the *definition of the situation*, familiar, that is, from his work on drama-turgy and strategic interaction. How is a particular definition of 'what is going on here and now' achieved and shored up by the things that people do with each other? How can these practices be made visible in the doings of daily life? Even a book like *Asylums* about which we will have a fair amount to say in a moment, can be seen to have the selfsame theme at its heart. Here the way it is brought out is by paying particular attention to the forms of interaction to be discerned between staff and inmates within the defined territory of the asylum itself. How is an appearance of rigid conformity and uniformity produced which at the same time allows the possibility of fine differentiations between individuals in institutional settings such as these? The ways of speaking about it may have changed but the central concern is still there.

The nature of the interest

The point of this chapter is not yet another textbook exposition of Goffman's work. It is, rather, to substantiate our claim that with a little effort, as well as sensitivity, Goffman's *sociological project* can be found to be a perfectly reasoned one, if not uncontentious. To do that we will have to take up some of the usual objections raised against his work and show that, by and large, they are based on misapprehensions.

The criticisms that have been made have mainly been directed at what are thought of as three fatal flaws in the work. First, it is said he promotes a cynical view of human nature, and a morality of selfishness and egocentricity. Goffman's is a Machiavellian sociology. Second, because of his view of the self, his work is partial and distorting. No one is really like a Goffmanesque person. Third, while his work is provocative and enjoyable to read, it is so idiosyncratic as to be completely non-replicable. You have to be Goffman to do Goffman-type work. The consequence of these flaws, it is thought, is that we should stop thinking of Goffman as a sociologist, stimulating and insightful though his work might be, and begin to consider him more as a social critic or essayist, an Emerson or Thoreau, as a social philosopher such as Santayana or William James, or as a social psychologist like Harry Stack Sullivan or George Herbert Mead.

What should we say about these criticisms? To start with, of course, it does not much matter either way what we call Goffman's work. We can label it social philosophy, social commentary, or anything else we think fit, *providing that it is the work that we pay attention to*. We shall not argue that, in the end, Goffman must and can only be seen as a sociologist. What we will say, though, is that it is possible to see in all of Goffman's work a constant preoccupation with classic and central problems in sociology. This is not to deny that he might demarcate these problems using concepts such as 'self', 'identity', and 'individual' which are normally encountered in psychology, or that he approaches these concepts by mobilising sets of ideas drawn from philosophically inclined writers such as Kenneth Burke, and seemingly arcane bodies of thought such as the branch of mathematical logic known as 'game theory'. But one way of seeing an underlying unity in all of this is to look for the *sociological* use that is made of them. What Goffman does is to take up central sociologically defined problems and explore them from a distinct sociological point of view.

The point that we are trying to bring out here is one which we have touched on many times. What distinguishes closely related intellectual pursuits such as sociology, psychology, and social philosophy is not always easy to identify. A lot of the time they seem to be talking about much the same things. But it is *how* they talk about them often where the difference can be found to lie. These different pursuits adopt what earlier we called different attitudes. Just as we can see different things in the woodyard (cf Ch. 2), so we might say that the sociological conception of an attitude towards self, identity, and so on, may vary considerably from that of psychology. This is not to prejudge any conclusions about inter- and intra-disciplinary relations, but to say, once again, that these are difficult and thorny matters which cannot be easily swept aside. At the heart of our suggestion that different general strategies for investigation, or *methodologies*. One consequence of this argument is that a great deal more sense could be made out of the turmoil sociology seems to be in, if we were to see the various tendencies, perspectives, or theoretical clusters as embodying attempts to follow through alternative methodological strategies. For exactly the same reason, what interests us is what Goffman does with the concepts he uses, not where they are supposed to have their home.

What the concept of 'self' designates in our ordinary talk is difficult to pin down. It would seem to involve at least the following three elements; a discrete conscious *individual* with a *personal biography* and a distinct *personality*. No doubt, were we to press harder, it would yield much more. But, at minimum, when we say of someone that they have self-confidence, self-knowledge, self-esteem, or whatever, we are saying something about a *person*. Accordingly, if Goffman's use of the term is seen as an attempt to depict and summarise what we ordinarily know about persons who have selves, no wonder we find it shallow and partial, and manipulative. The picture that Goffman offers in *The Presentation of Self*, *Stigma*, and *Strategic Interaction*, concerned as these are with strategies of information control, would be bound to make us all appear to be so much more egocentric, calculating, and lacking in the attributes of normal human decency than we know we actually are. To be sure we do have friends who are more selfish than others. But no one is selfish in everything, are they? No one is as self-absorbed, keen to be 'one up', constantly concerned to monitor other's reactions as Goffman makes us all out to be. If Goffman's description of the behaviour of interacting selves was supposed to be a description of what we know other people are like in daily life, then it would be both a distortion and an exaggeration. It would exclude the possibility of any residual goodness and humanity in people, as well as emptying social relations of any warmth and spontaneity.

But, of course, a characterisation of daily life as we all know it, is exactly what Goffman is not trying to give us. He is not concerned to picture the self as 'the-person-in-the-round'. He is not trying to show how we are all covering up what we are like 'underneath the façade', hiding in public what we know about ourselves in private and what we will have to face on the Day of Judgement. What Goffman is trying to do is make the self a visible, sociological phenomenon.

Goffman's naturalism

The way that Goffman chooses to make the self sociologically visible is to take up a particular methodological turn of thought. His is an attempt to promote the possibility of a 'naturalistic' sociology. The one thing that this does not mean is that Goffman wants to take over from the natural sciences a particular investigative aim such as the formulation of general laws, nor an explanatory strategy such as that of hypothetico-deductivism. Rather, what Goffman wants to adopt is a general attitude towards how one goes about making studies. The study of social relations need be very little different from the study of natural relations. It can involve exactly the same processes of collection, co-ordination, and categorising of forms of behaviour. Take the famous studies of animal communities like the herring-gull colony. All that the naturalist can see is activity, behaviour of one kind or another. To make sense of it all, the naturalist chooses to see it as expressing a multitude of solutions to a defined range of basic, instinctively given needs, food provision, reproduction, and so on. The behaviour is then presented in detail to show how it solves the problems. The bowing and scraping and fluttering are aggression displays made in defence of nesting territory; the pecking at the parent's bill is a stimulus to the regurgitation of food, and so on.

Out of what appears to be a chaos of activity, the naturalist finds an order which can only be demonstrated at the level of the detail of the behaviour. Goffman works in exactly the same way. Where the naturalist treats behaviour as the display of solutions set by basic needs, Goffman sees social behaviour as information exchange. The naturalist enables us to understand herring-gull behaviour by talking about it in ways that we are already familiar with, as courtship display or parental protection. Goffman operates in like vein except that he makes sense of things that we do by reference to other things that human beings do, our performances on stage, our participation in ceremonies, our playing of games, and our speaking of language. These are used as images to organise and categorise the behaviour that he observes 'naturalistically'. The naturalist's prime concern is the exposition of how the order which has been discerned is a response to the problems set in the natural environment, a response which is both instinctive and collective. To Goffman, the order which he notices, 'the interaction order', is a response to problems set in the social environment, and is, therefore, both social and collective in character. His naturalistic approach can be seen in the detailed nature of the observations he makes about operating theatres when an operation is taking place, the ways that 'con men' dispose of their 'mark' and the processes that inmates pass through as they become institutionalised.

We could, at this point, digress to discuss whether Goffman's 'naturalism' provides the basis for a 'proper' scientific methodology and how it is connected to the philosophy of pragmatism adopted by Dewy, James, and above all G H Mead. We could also explore the distinction between explanation and description as it relates to Goffman's work. These are important questions which would have to be part of any serious exposition of Goffman's work. But exposition is not our primary concern, and so these matters would not be strictly germane to our interest in delineating the nature of Goffman's socio-logical attitude. Rather than trace its origins, we will simply content ourselves with the observation that Goffman's sociology is predicated upon an investigative policy which we have dubbed 'naturalism'. This policy provides him with certain criteria of investigative relevance. It excludes anything which is not directly observable. Since all that the investigator can observe directly in social life is the behaviour of actors, this policy can fairly be called *methodological behaviourism*. The focus is always on what actors do and what can be said about what they do. If we now look at his books with this policy in mind, we can see that it is the way that he chooses to make the interaction order sociologically visible. That is to say, methodological behaviourism is a research strategy, not a philosophy of human nature. Goffman is not saying that people are simple 'behaving machines', nor is he saying that all that exists in the world is the sum total of objects and their behaviour. What he is doing is showing that the investigation of social life as social behaviour can be made to yield sociological insights and findings. In restricting his interests to behaviour, Goffman should not be read as saying there is behaviour and nothing else. It represents a point of view, a way of taking an interest in the self as observable behaviour. His books, from *The Presentation of Self*, through *Strategic Interaction* and *Frame Analysis*, to *Forms of Talk* deal with the dissection of the behaviour of interacting selves.

Once methodological behaviourism has been adopted, the diffi-culty is not with noticing things about social life, but with organising them into a coherent framework of observations. Central to the classic canon of sociological work is the exploration of the relationship between the individual and society. For sociology, individuals are members of collectivities, that is, individuals standing in social relationships. What makes this definition distinctively sociological is that the point of reference is taken as the collectivity rather than the individual. Individuals are discussed as individual members enmeshed in a wider system of social relationhips. Goffman brings his methodological behaviourism to this focal point. In doing so he develops a distinctive sociological view of the nature of social life, one that treats it as an 'interaction order'.

Methodological behaviourism allows Goffman to disregard questions about what lies behind behaviour, questions about what the behaviour 'really means'. All he is interested in is how what it means is displayed and understood in interaction. His behaviourism is not a theory of the mind nor of mental life. When he looks at the way we use scenes and settings, props and regions to find activities to have certain meanings, or how we ritualise the exchange of apologies, excuses, and other 'remedial interchanges' to prevent certain inferences being drawn from behaviour, he is looking at how behaviour is used to display and find meaning, and that is a sociological interest in meaning and not a psychological one.

The point of reference: 'the interaction order'

The basic elements of Goffman's approach, then, are these: (1) individuals are treated as being engaged in (2) a collectively organised (3) system of information exchange. Such information is made available and controlled in patterned and known-in-common ways. Just as Durkheim treats the individual in Aboriginal society as standing at a nexus of totemic relationships which express or represent the collective organisation of that society, so Goffman treats individuals as standing in the relationships of collectively organised information exchange distinctive of their societies. He enables us to see the sociological import of this by picking out the nature of this organisation by means of a number of carefully chosen images. One of these is the comparison of daily life with the theatre. The notion of *role* and role-playing *actors* is brought out by relating it to the milieu from which it was drawn. In treating social life as the performance of interacting roles, Goffman can ask about the conventions that are used to produce *recognisable and convincing performances*. How is this achieved in the course of giving a performance? To convey arrogance and hauteur, an actor may adopt a certain posture, tone of voice, facial movements. We can find someone to be arrogant simply in virtue of what they say and the way they say it, the way they 'look down their noses' at us and swagger around. We recognise and are convinced by the performance of arrogance both in daily life and when we see it on the stage.

The second image that Goffman uses is that of the game. The categories which this makes available are to be found in the vocabulary of strategies, ploys, rules, negotiation and bargaining, moves and counter-moves. The comparison is not now with the theatre but with the blackjack table and the Grand Masters' chessboard. How do we see a line of action as leading to an intended outcome, unfolding, modified, recast and abandoned? What are the standard 'moves' and the 'conventional strategies'? Goffman invites us to see such ordinary things as the line of action initiated by asking for a date, through the first kiss to 'going steady' and beyond as the unfolding of an interactional game in which there are moves and counter-moves, ploys, sub-ploys, bargains made, bids missed and conventional responses. Goffman is not saying that dating is just a game: he is saying that the socially organised character of dating can be made visible if you treat what people do as if they were playing a game. The third and fourth images which Goffman uses are much less well known and are on view in his later work. These are the comparison of selves with vehicular units and social life with traffic, and the comparison of the rules of social behaviour with the syntax for languages.

In looking at social life as the co-ordination of 'interchanges', Goffman asks how such encounters are managed by definitions of the environment or territory, the rules of social mobility, the singularity or otherwise of the units concerned, the signalling that is done and the signs that instruct us to behave in certain ways. What are the signs that 'tie' persons together or allow us to see them as separate? What are the various dimensions of 'social distance' and what are the consequences of violating them? Syntax is the use of rules for the production of acceptable sentences in any language. In asking what the syntax of daily life might be like, Goffman is taking up a theme that has become very popular in recent years, namely the treatment of social phenomena as symbols. The framework that is used is that of the distinction between 'keys' – the meanings of particular symbols that are in use; 'codes' – the organisation of those symbols; and 'frames' – the general grounds of meaning determination. An example may help here. Within the general frame of religious ritual, the particular rituals used by the Roman Catholic Church form a distinct code. They are both similar to and different from the rituals of other faiths. Part of many of those rituals is the burning of incense. This may once have had a practical point, large numbers of unwashed bodies in a small space can be off-putting. Today, however, we do not need to key in such a practical end. Instead we can see the rising of the clouds of incense as symbolic of the prayers of the faithful. We key it in entirely different ways. Goffman uses this idea to talk about how we achieve and display the keys, codes, and frames pertinent to daily life. We go into a church and expect certain things; we see distinctive 'vestments' and forms of behaviour; we see the particular meanings of the things that are done, people are blessed, communion is given, sermons are preached. When we are at home with our families, at the theatre, or in the classroom, different keys, codes, and frames apply.

In the various analyses, Goffman traverses the same terrain again and again. This is the range of settings in which the interaction order can be analysed. He lists them as the autonomous individual, the two-person encounter, the multi-person encounter, the platform performance, and the celebratory ritual. Although it condenses and oversimplifies his work, this idea of a two-dimensional array of forms of co-ordination and focus of analysis does display the essential continuity. Irreducibly the interaction order is a social order. This also helps to show why the third of the complaints made about Goffman can be discounted. Once Goffman has introduced and explored a different way of conceiving of this social order, there would seem to be little point in replicating it. What would be obtained other than more, probably inferior, Goffman-type studies? Goffman's systems of co-ordination and foci of analysis are not findings but heuristics. No one complains that it is impossible to replicate and validate Durkheim's proposition that crime is normal and functional in society because no one takes that to be a finding. It is, quite clearly, the demonstration of a sociological interest in the phenomenon of crime. The interest and the challenge is in working out more effectively, more elegantly, more precisely just how crime can or cannot be viewed in this way. The same holds for Goffman. Nothing is to be gained by applying his categories to novel areas, except perhaps the substantiation of their investigative fertility, if that were wanted. Expanding and extending Goffman's interest in social life would not be replication but the adoption of the same investigative policy – methodological behaviourism – and following of it through in wholly novel ways. That this has not been done is testimony to the sheer difficulty of making sociological innovations of the sort which Goffman achieved, not to the fact that you have to be Goffman to do studies like his.

Goffman's style

The comparison with Durkheim which we used just now could be open to challenge. People will respond that while Durkheim's basic *axiom* cannot be replicated and validated, the studies he carried out to demonstrate its truth can be. Indeed, his studies were designed so that they could be replicated, used as exemplars, and so on. But, we are not claiming that Goffman is through and through a Durkheimian, rather that in just this aspect they are comparable. Durkheim was wedded to a very clear notion of the scientific character of sociology. Its investigative techniques and the methods of presenting findings were to be modelled on the natural sciences. As we have seen, Goffman's investigative stance does match, in a rather limited way, that of one of the natural sciences. His methods of presentation do not. His is a 'literary' mode, not a 'scientific' one. It is this which makes his style so distinctive, for it is rhetorical rather than analytic, and it is rhetorical for a reason.

The distinction between rhetoric and analysis marks the difference between proffering explanations for phenomena and promoting sensibilities towards them. Explanations are the product of bodies of inferences which are arrived at by means of clearly defined procedures and rules. In sociology, as elsewhere, such inferences can be inductive or deductive, depending on the rules followed and the procedures adhered to. Making inferences is to engage in a certain kind of argument, but not the only kind. Attempts to convince us of the benefit, point, or need of something can proceed inferentially, or it can proceed in other ways. It can be made through an appeal to our better (or worse) natures, our hearts and minds, our loyalty, or, as in the case of Goffman, by the conviction that is carried in the detail of the observations. We are carried along by the flow and fascinated by the story, not convinced by his proof.

The presentational devices that Goffman uses are the images and metaphors referred to earlier and the building up of a collage of impressions from the sources used. This application of analogy and metaphor is in clear contrast to the theorising and modelling of other sociologists. Goffman's use of the image of the game is not 'game modelling'. He does not see the games he describes as simplified and rarified versions of social life. If anything, it is the other way around. Life is a simplified game. He does not build his model in advance in order to replicate only certain, predetermined features of social life. Rather, he jumbles everything together to see how the one illuminates the other. No procedural rules are offered to fix the degree of correspondence between games and 'reality', instead we are asked what it is about games that makes them really real as games. The observations are not formalised as a survey of the form under discussion; games, the theatre, traffic, languages, hospitals, hotels, drive-ins, backwards, etc. Out of the collage of impressions provided, the collage of sources quoted, the sense, the sensibility that Goffman is cultivating gradually emerges. As with all literary projects, there is some risk involved. People may be left cold, unable to see what all the fuss is about, or see in it something entirely different from that which Goffman intended. It is hard to imagine someone seeing something in *Suicide* other than what Durkheim intended. That is both its strength and its weakness. For Goffman, the riskiness of his literary mode is its strength. But it also enables misapprehension and misunderstanding.

ASYLUMS

With all of these things in mind, how might one approach a particular book of Goffmans, say the most famous of them all, *Asylums*? First and foremost, we would be wise to go slowly and not to assume that because the book features certain kinds of organisational settings, it is only about those settings. *Stigma* is not only, or even primarily about the crippled and the handicapped, the diseased, and the socially outcast, and *Asylums* is not solely about prisons, mental hospitals, army barracks, and boarding schools. Both are exercises in sociological reasoning using the resources and settings they do as materials. Such materials are deliberately chosen for the way in which they throw into relief the very ordinary social processes which are also the object of concern. *Asylums* is not best read as an indictment of custodial mental hospitals and the prison system, even though Goffman certainly does have some harsh things to say about the consequences of many of the practices adopted in these places. Such 'total institutions' are settings in which collectively defined social identities are projected and imposed upon the individual. But individuals are not automatons, they respond to and cope with such processes of definition. The node of the book is the classic tension between the demands of the collectivity and the expression of individuality; a tension not just to be found in prisons and hospitals but throughout society. From the point of view of each one of us, society is a constraining reality that we both have to recognise and come to terms with.

The Durkheimian motif to the inmates' situation is drawn out in various ways. The general features of the inmates' world, the penetration of the organisational nature of the institution into all facets of life is documented at length. We are shown how the separateness of the institution from the outside world is impressed upon the individual through rituals of mortification and profanation, the loss of privacy and self-responsibility and determination, the enforcing of routine, the wearing of uniforms, and identification by number and file. Gradually the inmate takes over the institutional culture; the rules and systems of privilege and reward are learned, the 'lingo' and 'dodges', who can be trusted and who not. This transformation of self-identity is a process which Goffman calls a 'moral career', a term resonating with Durkheim's definition of society as a moral order, since it involves a change in the criteria against which one judges others and oneself. The relevant standards are 'inmate' ones, not those of the 'outside'. Using as his leading example, mental patients, Goffman tracks this process through its various stages and points out the significant role that close relatives have in beginning the process of social isolation that leads to commitment to the institution, the ways that life histories are constructed and reconstructed in the light of the unfolding of events as patients 'become mentally ill'. Strategically important in this process, is the loss of control that the patient experiences over potentially discrediting information about himself. Job failures, marriage break-ups are on the file and could become common knowledge. Resentment and non-acceptance of inmate status become symptomatic of a lack of realism and indicate potentiality for disruptive behaviour that has to be controlled. Hospital authorities and the patient's kin form coalitions to control the inmate's behaviour.

Just as Durkheim suggested that social order in society depended upon the definition and continual reaffirmation of a moral boundary between the sacred and the profane, attention to the 'underlife' of a total institution, Goffman suggests, will show that the institution's profanation of self by the forced collectiveness of social life ensures that the boundary will be drawn elsewhere, around the privacy of the letters which inmates keep in their lockers, and possessions they carry in their pockets, the work and therapy tasks they are assigned to, and the wards and wings they find themselves on. These come to have a sacred character which, if threatened, is defended out of all proportion to its apparent worth. Patients insist on carrying all their belongings around in a blanket, fighting over who is to be first to have their medicine and are angered at any disruption of routine. In addition a whole infrastructure of rights and obligations, an economy of traded goods and earnings, gambling schools, alliances and liaisons emerge. These secondary adjustments to the totality of institutional life are how the inmates redraw the moral boundary and cope with daily life.

The parallel with Durkheim can be made even more forcibly. Durkheim was well aware that the individuals making up society are not automatons or clones. They act for their own reasons, on their own initiative, and differ from one another in a myriad of ways. But they are social individuals in that they share a pattern of life which is collaborative. In accommodating to the collectively expressed demands of others, some social space in which to express that individuality is a necessity. Thus is it in total institutions as well. As Goffman puts it, in the interstices of the organisation men are able to live out their lives and retain a sense of their own identity through the pictures they put on their walls, the contents of their lockers, and the slight alterations they make to the clothes they wear.

Asylums is an exercise in sociology. It reflects clear sociological interests. Although it is not easy to locate in the simplified matrix suggested earlier, nevertheless, it falls fairly and squarely in the general field which Goffman has circumscribed for himself. What is examined is the collective nature of social life as that is made visible by observation of what people do. *Asylums* does not lie at the intercept of the two aces of the matrix, but ranges across both. In the classical sense, it is a sociological treatise, a point which those who read it simply as a book on mental hospitals and prisons, a diatribe against custodial institutions, are likely to miss.

CONCLUSION

The conclusion of this chapter can well stand as the conclusion for the whole book. Reading sociology can be stimulating, rewarding, and exciting, but to be so requires expending some time and exacting effort. The more practised one is in playing a game, the easier it is to mask the effort and give the appearance of grasping what is going on. Goffman, as ever, offers a cameo of just this phenomenon in his paper on 'Role Distance'. Because playing the game requires effort and patience, we should not be misled by the facility and sureness of those who play it well. Their ease is the outcome of years of practice. Similarly, we should not be misled into thinking that the homilies, the arguments, the ideas, the advice, and so on, presented in this book will circumvent the need for effort on the part of aspiring sociologists. Obviously, we hope to have given such guidance so that sense can be made of what sociologists are trying to do. But the difficulties we have identified should also indicate that making sense of what sociologists are trying to do by no means solves the problems and the difficulties with which the subject has to deal. It is only a first step. Mastering the game requires patient effort and lots of practice.

Sociology embodies lots of choices of how to play. There are still many things to be done, arguments to follow through, empirical areas to be investigated: all offering a challenge both to newcomers and to those who have long acquaintance with it. It challenges newcomers to master the 'games' presently on offer. It challenges the rest of us to question old and familiar habits of thought to look for novel and innovative ways of thinking about and investigating social life. At this stage of its development there is no necessity to treat sociology as if it were seeking to find the one and only correct description and explanation of the social world. For us, it is much more valuable to preserve the variety it already exhibits. This is one reason why we have emphasised the argumentative nature of the discipline and the choices open to us in the way of theorising and investigating social life. Retaining this sense of variety will, so we hope, mean that we are less likely to disregard ideas but treat them with the charity they deserve as efforts to say something sociologically worthwhile even if they are not our preferences. We can, indeed will, have preferences, prefer Marxism to Functionalism, Ethnomethodology to Symbolic Interactionism, Durkheim to Weber, and so on, but to adopt a preference does not mean that we have to regard other preferences as unreasoned, crass, distorted, or even wrong. The best way to support a sociological preference surely is to follow its arguments through, show that it works, answer the questions it sets out to answer, making it something that is sociologically exciting and worthwhile: in short, mastering the 'game'.

FURTHER READING

J DITTON (ed.), *The View from Goffman*, Blackwell, 1981. One of the few attempts to take Goffman seriously as a social theorist.

E GOFFMAN, *The Presentation of Self in Everyday Life*, Pelican, 1959; *Encounters*, Bobs Merril, 1961; *Stigma*, Pelican, 1968; *Interaction Ritual*, Penguin, 1967; *Relations in Public*, Pelican, 1971; *Frame Analysis*, Peregrine, 1975; *Forms of Talk*, Blackwell, 1981. These are among his works referred to.

INDEX